R U a teenage health freak?

AIDAN MACFARLANE and ANN McPHERSON

OXFORD
UNIVERSITY PRESS

OXFORD
UNIVERSITY PRESS

Great Clarendon Street, Oxford OX2 6DP

Oxford University Press is a department of the University of Oxford.
It furthers the University's objective of excellence in research, scholarship,
and education by publishing worldwide in

Oxford New York

Auckland Bangkok Buenos Aires Cape Town Chennai
Dar es Salaam Delhi Hong Kong Istanbul Karachi Kolkata
Kuala Lumpur Madrid Melbourne Mexico City Mumbai Nairobi
São Paulo Shanghai Taipei Tokyo Toronto

Oxford is a registered trade mark of Oxford University Press
in the UK and in certain other countries

British Library Cataloguing in Publication Data available

ISBN 0-19-910916-8

1 3 5 7 9 10 8 6 4 2

Printed in Great Britain
by Cox & Wyman Ltd, Reading, Berkshire.

Contents

SEX – THE UPS AND DOWNS

There is much more to sex than just...sex

'Sex' does not necessarily mean having sexual intercourse. There are many, many things people can do (and do do!) which are extremely sexy that do not necessarily involve having actual sexual intercourse. It's when the man puts his penis into a woman's vagina that the worries start – 'help, pregnancy!' or 'help, sexually transmitted infections!'

Some of these things can be done alone, like masturbation, and others with a partner. Whatever kind of sex you have, it should be fun, safe, respectful of the other person's wishes, and enjoyable on both sides. And ideally it should happen within a good relationship.

● ## THE FIRST COURSE

Dear Dr Ann – **I've recently started to go out with someone** and people are trying to force us to kiss and they're calling me frigid but the only thing is i just feel uncomfortable kissing my girlfriend in front of others. What's wrong with me?!

Dear 'Reluctant public kisser' – Absolutely nothing is wrong with you. It's completely normal to only want to show affection in private. It sounds like you're being bullied. It is the warmth of feeling that you show to your girlfriend in private that matters. You know how you feel about this girl, so don't go getting bullied by others – it is your life and the way that you feel about how you want to live it.

Dear Dr Ann – **I have this habit of letting guys feel my breasts.** The reason I'm worried is that I quite enjoy it. I'm worried I might take it too far. What should I do?

Dear 'Person worried that things might go too far' – It's not surprising that you like having your breasts touched. Breasts are very sensuous organs, and they will have an effect on your body generally and make you feel sexually aroused. Just make sure you don't put yourself in a situation where things can get out of hand. And by the way, don't just let just any guy touch them – only those you really like.

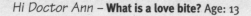

Hi Doctor Ann – **What is a love bite?** Age: 13

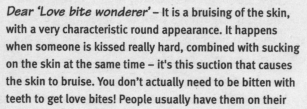

Dear 'Love bite wonderer' – It is a bruising of the skin, with a very characteristic round appearance. It happens when someone is kissed really hard, combined with sucking on the skin at the same time – it's this suction that causes the skin to bruise. You don't actually need to be bitten with teeth to get love bites! People usually have them on their neck, and they take a week or so to clear. Be sure to tell anyone who is kissing you like this to stop if you don't like it.

● R U READY 4 THE INTER COURSE ?

Surveys of young people's first sexual experiences indicate that by the age of 16 about one in four girls and one in three boys have had sexual intercourse. Or to put it the other way round, three out of four girls and two out of three boys have not had sexual intercourse. Some young people (more girls than boys) regret their first sexual experience. You need to make sure your first sex is at a time you want and with someone you want, rather than an accident – like being too drunk to say 'no' to someone you have just met at a party. But remember, having sex with anyone under the age of 16 is illegal.

Dear Dr Ann – **How do I know if I am ready for sex?**

Dear 'Ready for sex?' – I don't know how old you are, but there is no rush. First, being 'ready for sex' and 'being ready for sexual intercourse' are two very different things. The average age at which young people start on 'sex' – like kissing, touching, holding and feeling – is around 13 years. As far as sexual intercourse is concerned, two out of three boys and three out four girls DON'T have sexual intercourse till they are over 16, so there should be no pressure. And remember that having sexual Intercourse with a girl who is less than 16 years old is illegal. Perhaps the two main things are (a) to know what you are doing – check out the info on sex contraception and body changes in chapters 6 and 8; and (b) not to be pressurized by anyone else into doing anything that you don't want to do.

Dear Dr Ann – **How do I know if I am still a virgin?** Girl 16.

Dear 'Virgin questioner' – You stop being a virgin once you have had actual sexual intercourse – where the man's penis actually enters the girl's vagina, even if only for a little way. This definition applies whether you are a girl or a boy. In girls the way into the vagina is covered by a very, very thin skin called the 'hymen', which gets completely broken during sexual intercourse. Before it gets broken, there are little holes in it that allow vaginal and menstrual discharge to get through. The hymen sometimes gets torn naturally when the girl does sports or uses a tampon, but this doesn't mean that you are not a virgin.

Dear Dr Ann – **I'm thinking of having sex. Will I get pregnant from the first time?**

Dear 'Person thinking of having sex for the first time' – You can get pregnant any time that you have sex – the first, second or three hundred and thirtieth time. If you don't want to get pregnant, always use a contraceptive – preferably a condom, or a condom and the pill. The condom will also stop you catching any nasty sexually transmitted infection. Check out the facts in chapter 6.

Dear Dr Ann – **I'm nearly fifteen, and I have a sixteen-year-old boyfriend.** The problem is, he wants sex, and I want sex, but I'm under age, and sometimes I want it like hell, and the rest of the time I'm scared. Also, I'm not the most experienced girl in the world, so I really don't know what to do about anything.

Dear 'Person nearly 15 and wanting to have sex' – the first thing you need to know is that having sexual intercourse when you are under the age of 16 is illegal. But you probably know that already. It is good that you are not 'experienced'– there is the rest of your life to become 'experienced' in. It sounds to me as if you are not yet ready to have sexual intercourse, so why not hold off, stick to saying 'no' and try all the other nice sexy things that you can do without actually having intercourse. Meanwhile get well informed about contraception. The Family Planning Association do some great leaflets and have a phone line – their phone number is 0845 310 1334 (free line).

Dear Dr Ann – **I fancy a lad but all he wants is sex.** I really like him to be my boyfriend. At the moment I have had sex with him with condoms but he wants to take it a step further. What shall I do? Lass 15.

Dear 'Lad fancier' – If 'taking it a step further' means NOT using condoms, DON'T DO IT. And remember, if you are under 16, it is illegal to have sex anyhow. Sounds to me as if he just wants sex, and surely you want something more out of the relationship than just that?

Dear Dr Ann – **What if I'm having sex and instead of semen I just pee?** I know it sounds stupid but I have nightmares about it. I mean, think of the look on her face when she realizes – oh, God, it's too awful to think about.

Dear 'Worrier about semen versus pee' – If your penis is erect enough to have sex, it's too erect to pee. A valve shuts your bladder off so that only sperm gets through. So don't lose any more sleep about it. If there's some pee still in the tubes, your body

cleans up the tube in your penis (the urethra) before you ejaculate. Urine is too acid for sperm, you see, so as you're getting excited, your body sends a dab of clear pre-ejaculatory fluid through your penis to get rid of any traces of urine. It comes out as a little droplet at the end of your penis.

SEXUALLY TRANSMITTED INFECTIONS

Sexually transmitted infections are infections that can be passed on when having sexual intercourse. There are some sexually transmitted diseases that you can get by having other kinds of sex. Whatever kind of sex you are having, condoms will almost always stop you getting a sexually transmitted infection.

Dear Dr Ann – **This is so embarrassing I'm not going to sign it** but I'm desperate. I get really stinky down there sometimes, it's like bad French cheese. And my knickers get all stained. I think I must have an infection or a disease or something. What's wrong with me? from Me.

Dear 'Person with smelly knickers' – Staining your knickers is usually due to a discharge from your vagina. This can happen when you start having your periods – it is your hormones telling the cells in the wall of your vagina to produce more sticky stuff called mucus. Some discharge is normal, but it shouldn't smell bad. So, first check – could you have left a tampon in? The next commonest trouble is when your vagina gets infected with a yeast called candida, which especially likes living in mouths and vaginas. You often get it after taking antibiotics. It makes your vagina very itchy and you get a discharge that looks like cottage cheese (no chives, though). Luckily, candida is easy to treat. You can get a cream and tablets called Clotrimazone. The cream you put around the edge of your vaginal opening, the tablets you put into your vagina. Or pop along to your doctor and get it checked out first if you're worried – you can ask to see a woman doctor if you are embarrassed having a male one check you out.

Dear Dr Ann – **My boyfriend has red spots on his penis under his foreskin.** He also said that at times he needs to go to the toilet, but when he gets there he can't go. He said that it isn't painful. Could this be herpes? We haven't had sex for about a week and this has only been noticed a few days ago – please help

Dear 'Girl with red-spotted boyfriend' – The first thing to say to any girl in this situation is to stay away from boys with red spots on their penises. But seriously, he needs to go and see his doctor, or to a specialist at a Genito-urinary Clinic, to find out what the spots are. Yes, they could be herpes or some other sexually transmitted infection. Then you need to get checked out as well. You don't say whether you have been using condoms or not. But using condoms is the best way of being as sure as you can that those red spots don't spread to you!

Dear Dr Ann – **Can you die from chlamydia?**

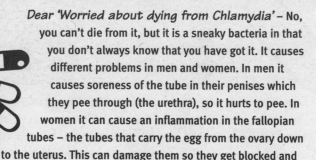

Dear 'Worried about dying from Chlamydia' – No, you can't die from it, but it is a sneaky bacteria in that you don't always know that you have got it. It causes different problems in men and women. In men it causes soreness of the tube in their penises which they pee through (the urethra), so it hurts to pee. In women it can cause an inflammation in the fallopian tubes – the tubes that carry the egg from the ovary down to the uterus. This can damage them so they get blocked and the woman can't have babies. It can also cause inflammation of the neck of the woman's womb and give a vaginal discharge. If you are worried you have caught it, get checked out by a doctor as it is easily treated with antibiotics. Use a condom when you have sexual intercourse and you are unlikely to catch it!

Dear Dr Ann – **What are the main causes of AIDS/HIV?**

Dear 'Wanting to know about causes of AIDS/HIV' – 'AIDS' stands for Acquired Immune Deficiency Syndrome. This is the disease caused by the virus HIV

(Human Immunodeficiency Virus), which affects the body's immune system. You can be infected by HIV but not be ill, as it takes time for the virus to cause the illness. But even though you are not ill, you can still pass the virus on to someone else and infect them, so that in time they will also develop Aids. The commonest way that people in the UK catch HIV is by having sexual intercourse with someone who has already been infected by the virus. This can be between a man and woman or between two men. Another way people catch the virus is by injecting drugs with a needle that has already been used by someone who has the infection or the disease.

If you are worried that you may have a sexually transmitted infection, here are some useful UK phone numbers:
- Family Planning Association Helpline – 0845 310 1334 (free phone), open 9 a.m. to 7 p.m., Monday to Friday
- Brook Advisory Service, Young People's Helpline – 0800 0185 023
- Sexwise – Helpline 0800 282930

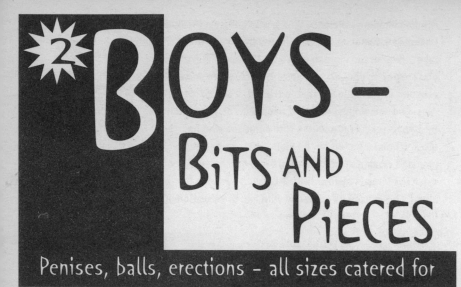

2 BOYS –
BiTS AND
PiECES

Penises, balls, erections – all sizes catered for

Penises come in many shapes and sizes, some circumcised, others not, some longer and some shorter, some curved, some straight, some pointing upwards when erect, others downwards when erect. But they all contain special tissue which fills with blood when you are sexually stimulated and which causes the penis to lengthen and become hard. The size of the penis, whether soft or hard, varies considerably between individuals and between men of different races. But when it comes to sex, it is not the length or thickness that matters so much as the kind of person the owner of the penis is and the kind of relationship the people having the sex have with one another.

● **WILLIES– BIG, SMALL, STRAIGHT, CURVED**

Dear Dr Ann – **What is the average size of a penis?** Worried aged 13.

Dear 'Average penis wonderer' – You will be glad to hear that there is information on this. The first thing to say is that there is a huge variation in the size of the unerect penis of boys and men. Some doctors in the USA measured the unerect penises of a large number of boys at different ages (see below). Or you can send a stamped addressed envelope to the Family Planning Association, 2–12 Pentonville Rd, London, N1 9FP (it's free!).

Ask for the leaflet called '4 Boys – a below the belt guide to the male body'. It's terrific and contains lots of facts about balls, penises, scrotums and masturbation.

An American doctor did some research and found that the normal floppy size for 10 year olds is 4-8 cm, for 12 year olds is 5-10 cm, for 14 year olds is 6-14 cm, for 16 year olds is 10-15 cm, and for 18 year olds is 11-17 cm. However, he also found that however small the floppy size is, over 90% of men grow to between 14-18 cm when erect.

Dear Dr Ann – **i am really worried about my penis size.** how can i make it bigger without surgery??

Dear 'Penis size worrier' – Many boys and men are, like you, worried about the size of their penis – but how big is big enough? There is variation in penis size just as there is variation in people's overall size. Also there is no known way of making your penis bigger, and though some boys claim that the more you masturbate, the bigger it gets, there is no evidence that this works. Like the size of the rest of you, you will have to learn to live with what you've got and – what is equally important – to enjoy it. If you do, then so will others who come into contact with it!

Dear Dr Ann – **My willy is 12 inches long.** Is this normal as I worry that I could really hurt a girl with it.
Dear Dr Ann – **I've got 10 inches down there**, is this normal? Yours, Bigboy
Dear Dr Ann – **I'm massively well endowed** and can't find trousers to fit...

Dear 'Showing off your size' lads. Are you trying to tell me about a medical problem or how well hung you are? If you really are 12 inches long, then congratulations, but I doubt it's true! Read the surveys – the girls all say it's the bloke behind the penis that counts. You're also miraculously in 0.01% of the population.

Dear Dr Ann – **My penis is a lot smaller than the average size,** can you tell me what to do, please, please help me, I am really scared but daren't go to the doctor. I have entered puberty but the size of my penis has never increased. I am 17 years old and will be 18 in the summer. The size of my penis is 4 cm floppy and about 7 cm erect. I am too embarrassed to go the toilet in a restaurant in case anyone is looking.

Dear 'Worried about your penis size' – You really, really need to get your courage up. Worrying about the size of your penis won't make it grow longer. You say that you have other signs of puberty, but before helping in any way, someone would need to know all the details – things like whether you have pubic hair or hair under your arms, and whether your balls have grown enough. You will have to pluck up courage and see a doctor face to face – it is the only way to know for certain.

Dear Dr Ann – **i have a curved penis** and i'm really worried if it is normal and about having sex in case i hurt the girl, will it be ok?

Dear 'One with the curve' – A bit of a curve is not all that uncommon, but for most men it doesn't affect them having sex, and doesn't hurt the girl. There is a very rare condition called 'Peyronies disease', where there is band of fibrous tissue that makes the penis markedly curved when erect. If you are worried, have a doctor look at it and advise you.

Dear Dr Ann – **I am 14, and I have this brown mark down the underside of my penis.** It looks like a really large vein, but it doesn't feel like one. What should I do?

Dear 'Person with brown mark on penis' – I don't think that you have anything to worry about here. Many men have a line on the underside of their penis which is browner than the rest of the skin of their penis. It is usually in a fairly straight line and stretches all along the middle underneath.

...WITH KNOBS ON

Just as the size and shape of your penis as a whole varies hugely, so does the glans or knob – the very sensitive dome at the end of the penis. When a boy baby is born, the standard penis comes with a foreskin, which covers the sensitive end. For some people, like Jews and Muslims, it is standard practice to remove this bit of skin and leave the end of the penis exposed. This is called circumcision.

Dear Dr Ann – **my Mr penis has been hurting on the end** for 2 days now, what is wrong with it?

Dear 'Person with Mr Penis hurting' – If you haven't had sex, then the most likely cause is either a lot of masturbation, or an infection caused by a yeast called candida –more commonly known as 'thrush'. This makes the end your penis go red, sore and itchy. It sometimes happens when you have been on antibiotics.
If you think it is thrush, go and see your doctor, who will give you a prescription for some special antifungal cream, which will clear it up easily. You can also buy it over the counter at the chemist's. Doctors look at penises all the time, so don't feel embarrassed. If you have had sex, then you must go and get checked out to make sure that you haven't got a sexually transmitted infection.

Dr Ann – **My foreskin is quite tight** and I have trouble pulling it over my penis when erect. What should I do?

Dear 'Tight foreskin owner' – Many men cannot pull their foreskin back over the glans of their penis when they are erect. If you can pull your foreskin back over the glans of your penis when you are NOT erect, you have nothing to worry about. The one sign of having a foreskin that is too tight is if you have problems when peeing – and your foreskin balloons out as you start.

Dear Dr Ann – **What is knob cheese?** Some of my mates were joking about it – is it just a joke or is it real?

Dear 'Knob cheese wonderer' – It's not a joke but don't worry too much, because almost all men who are uncircumcised get a greasy substance called 'smegma' under their foreskin. It is made up of dead skin cells –

which come off all parts of your body all the time, like when your skin gets flaky or you get dandruff on your head. The stuff on your knob is mainly greasy secretions from glands in the skin folds at the end of your penis. All you need to do is to regularly pull your foreskin back gently and wash the stuff off.

Dear Dr Ann – **I have a purple vein-like ring at the bottom of my penis head.** As I am too embarrassed to ask a friend or family, please tell me if this is normal.

Dear 'Purple-ringed penis owner' – This 'vein-like ring' around the base of the glans of your penis is completely normal. There is normally a whole network of veins at the base of the glans. Like the veins on the back of your hand, these are more obvious in some people than others. However, these veins are much more obvious when you have been circumcised and when your penis is erect.

● ALL ABOUT BALLS

Your balls or bollocks (testes) are there to produce sperm. This starts when you reach puberty. They need to hang outside the body because otherwise they get too hot to produce sperm.

Dear Dr Ann – **Please I need help. My balls haven't yet dropped and i'm 16.**

Dear '16-year-old ball worrier' – We all tend to vary a bit in our development, but in roughly 95 out of every 100 boys, their balls have started to enlarge and drop down by the age of 14. If you cannot feel your balls at all, you should go and get checked by your doctor NOW. If it's just that they have not grown large yet, then you could go down to your doctor at a more leisurely pace and have them checked!

Dear ...
the sac and was in ...
it and pushed it back in now ...
testicle...i am scared i will not be able to have ...
help...

Dear 'Yoyo testicle' – In some men the testicles go up into the groin from time to time and then come down again. The very fact that your testicles come down into your sac is good news, because any boy/man whose testes do not come down does need to see a doctor. But if your testicle goes on aching, do please go and see your doctor anyhow. Now as for being able to make babies – if your testicles come down into your sac, they should be able to make babies fine.

Dear Dr Ann – **i am 14 and i am slightly worried about this thing by my left ball.** i know it's usual for it to hang lower than the other but i have this sort of spongy out of shape thing that i am worried about. Please help, and please don't tell me i have 2 go to a doctor?! Age: 14

Dear 'Worried about left ball' – One ball does normally hang lower than the other. The spongy out-of-shape thing you ask about is probably a little knot of veins (blood vessels) near your testes. I'm going to suggest that you should go to see a doctor as it's very difficult to be absolutely sure without actually checking it out.

Dear Dr Ann – **I was desperate to snog my girlfriend the other day but couldn't.** But then I got this stiffy and really, really bad ache in my bollocks. Is there something wrong with me?

Dear 'Ball acher' – No, nothing wrong here. Men can get a bad ache in their balls – and often in their groin too – when they are sexually excited but don't go any further. We don't know the exact reason why, but it seems to get particularly bad when they start kissing, get sexually aroused, but then don't go any further. But this is absolutely no excuse for trying to get a girl to go further!

Dear Dr Ann
left testi...
bar...

Dr Ann – a while ago one of my t...
my groin a couple of day...
time to time...

...to see a ...uld be checked out quickly just in case it is something serious, like testicular cancer. This has an almost 100% cure rate if it is caught early. But you absolutely must remember that most lumps or irregularities in the testes will not be cancer.

These are the things to look out for in your testes after puberty and to get checked by a doctor if they happen:

- a testicle dragging or feeling heavy
- a dull ache
- a testis getting bigger after the normal increase in size at puberty
- a small hard lump
- a change in shape or size

Dear Dr Ann – **this is soooo embarrassing** that i cant go to the doctor or talk to no1 about it so i am writing 2 u. **My balls are wonky** – with 1 a bit bigger than the other.

Dear 'Wonky balls' - most men's balls are a bit lopsided. One is bigger than the other or one hangs lower than the other. How high or low they hang also depends on how hot it is. If it is cold, they shrink closer to your body to keep warm, and if it's hot, they'll tend to hang loose. It's all to keep your sperm in tip-top condition. Having one side lower than the other also stops them banging into one another when you're running around.

Dear Dr Ann - **I'm 14. My**
red, saw and the skin is peeling. Please
please help me as i don't know what is wrong?

> *Dear 'Person with 'saw' scrotum'* – Ouch, that sounds
> really sore. You and I are both glad that there is something that
> can be done about it. Most likely is that you have a fungal infection –
> a bit like athlete's foot but on your scrotum. You could get down to the
> chemist for some anti-fungal cream, and it should soon be as good as new.
> But it would be best to get it checked out by your doc first and then you could get
> the cream free with a prescription. There's no need to be embarrassed – doctors are
> used to checking out all parts of the body!

Dear Dr Ann – **if i get punched in the ball will it stop me from producing sperm**
again?

> *Dear 'Punched balls'* – The main problem with getting
> punched balls is just how incredibly painful it is (as you
> may have already discovered!). Sometimes after being
> kicked or punched in the balls, they may become
> swollen, bruised and feel very tender. This may last for a
> few days, and wearing Y-fronts, which give you some
> support, helps this tenderness. Almost all men get
> bashed in the balls sometime in their life, so if it
> stopped sperm production, there wouldn't be any babies
> around! You'll be fine.

● HARD-ONS, BONERS, STIFFIES

Dear Dr Ann – **I'm 12 and now when I wake up I've got a stiffy**
every morning. What's wrong?

> *Dear 'Person with a morning stiffy'* – Nothing wrong here,
> you're just a normal bloke! Most blokes get erections in their
> sleep without noticing. It wears off a minute or two after they
> wake up. It doesn't mean you're a sex maniac – as I'm sure you
> know, erections often pop up when you're not thinking about sex
> at all.

...this way of checking
...eous erections 'out of the
...e is little you can do about it other
...sit down, or turn away from your

Dear Dr Ann - **I don't think I'm gay but I get an erection in the showers** at school with the other guys. Then they laugh at me and call me gay, what can I do? What if I am really gay?

Dear 'Boner in the shower' – Getting an erection when you're surrounded by lots of naked bods – men or women – is normal. It doesn't mean you're gay but does mean that your brain is just thinking of sex in general, and that's what gives you an erection. Whether you are gay or not is something you have to figure out for yourself over time. Around 6 in every 100 blokes have some kind of gay experience sometime, somewhere, but only about 1 in 100 adult men would say they were gay.

Dear Dr. Ann – **my question is i have something wrong with my penis** and i am scared to have sex in case i have something wrong with me. underneath my penis i have a few weird spots (white ones but not pussy) – can you tell me if there is anything wrong with me please? 16 male.

Dear 'Faulty penis speculator' – The spots on your penis that are bothering you are nothing to worry about . They are little glands that produce greasy stuff called sebum. Try not to squeeze them in case they get infected. They are normal and all men have them. They do not mean you have any sort of infection that can be passed on when you have sex.

The regular, standard-issue penis comes with many different types of lumps and bumps, most of which are entirely normal and innocent. What come as part of the standard equipment are bumps like the ones you get all over your scrotum (ball bag) – though there they come with hairs growing out of them. They are round, slightly raised whitish lumps about 1 millimetre across, and they are mainly on the underside of the penis. Sometimes these have a little greasy stuff in them when you squeeze them, and hairs grow out of them towards the base of the penis.

Warts on the penis feel hard and a bit 'gritty' and tend to be odd-shaped. They are caused by a virus. Twenty per cent of warts disappear within a year without you doing anything about them but if you have warts on your penis always get them checked by a doctor.

Dear Dr Ann – **I have got some wart-type lumps on my penis.**

Dear 'Warty penis owner' – Warts on your penis are small fleshy growths, and look a bit like the kind of wart that you may get on your fingers. They feel hard and often have an uneven cauliflower-like surface, and they can be very small. There may be just one or you can have lots, and they tend not to hurt. It is very rare to get them unless you have had sexual intercourse, but the warts may not appear until up to a year after you have had sex! Always have them checked out, as you can get rid of them with a special 'paint' and also because they may be associated with another sexually transmitted infection.

Dear Dr Ann – **What are sperms made of?**

Dear 'Curious about human sperm' – Each individual sperm is made up of three parts – the head, the middle and the tail. Think of it as a missile ready to launch. The head is the missile's warhead and contains the chromosomes – the genetic material needed to develop into a baby if the sperm fertilizes an egg. Normal cells have 46 chromosomes, but a sperm cell has only half that number, 23, as does a woman's egg cell (ovum). So when a sperm meets up and joins with an egg, the fertilized egg has the full 46 chromosomes. The middle bit of the sperm is very complicated and controls the sperm's activities. The tail is like a propeller and speeds the sperm to its target – the egg. The rest of what a man ejaculates – about a teaspoonful altogether – is made up of water, sugar, protein, vitamin C, zinc and prostaglandins.

The sperm story, or how to populate China all on your own

Once you have started to produce sperm, you make up to a 1000 million a day. It takes over two months to make a sperm, but as you are making them all the time, you won't run out. An individual sperm is tiny, and each time you ejaculate, your 'cum' contains about 300 million of them. The semen that you ejaculate and which contains the sperm is a thick, slightly gelatinous fluid with a grey, whitish or creamy colour.

3 GIRLS – AND BiTS OF THEIR BITS AND PiECES

What it looks like down there

Some of girls' bits are rather less obvious than boys' bits. The most obvious ones – breasts – you can find out about in the next chapter. Looking at the more hidden bits (which, if you are their owner, you can do using a mirror), first there are the outer lips, called the labia majora, which run from the clitoris at the front to the anus (bum hole) at the back. These can vary in size and, after puberty, are often hairy on the outside. They swell up when you get sexually excited. Inside are your inner lips, the labia minora, which are thinner and don't have hair on them. Between these lips is your clitoris at the front, then your urethral opening (the hole you pee out of), then your vaginal opening, and then your anus.

● ABOUT YOUR VAGINAL LIPS

Dear Dr Ann – ok this is a majorly embarrassing thing to ask but its been worrying me so i'll have to do it. I noticed that **one of the lips of my vagina is bigger than the other one** and hangs out. I was worried about this because i think that no boy is going to want to touch me and they are going to think i'm weird. is this normal??

19

Dear 'Worried about being normal' – You don't need to worry about the lips of your vagina being different sizes. Quite a lot of girls notice that one side is bigger than the other – this is completely normal. Boys' balls are often different sizes and hang at different levels, and there's nothing weird about that either.

Dr Ann – i have an embarrassing problem with down below. **my bits have swelled up** + i don't want 2 tell no1. i'm a virgin so it's not STD. PS – i'm a girl.

Dear 'Girl with swollen bits' – There are several things that it could be. It could be an allergy caused by a spray or lotion. So don't use a spray, lotion or potion, and steer clear of any vaginal deodorants. Next you could have an infection – which in your case obviously can't be sexually transmitted. If you are sore and itchy, it could be thrush, or if it is just on one side, it may be a cyst. Sounds as if it would be a good idea to get it checked out by a doctor or nurse at school or at your local practice – anything you say to them will be absolutely confidential.

● VAGINAL DISCHARGE

It is quite normal for girls to have some vaginal discharge, which increases at the time of puberty as the mucous glands in your vagina get active in response to your hormones. The discharge can be clear or creamy white.

Dear Dr Ann – **I'm just curious as to what exactly is a normal discharge?** All the descriptions I've heard have been pretty vague. I can get quite bad smelling discharge, which sometimes looks as if it has a weird texture like jelly, and it can range in colour from clear to white to a greeny-yellow colour. Is this normal and what exactly does the discharge look like when you have an infection? Signed X a 15 year old girl.

Dear 'Curious about vaginal discharge' – Girls start to increase the amount of discharge they produce as they go through puberty and the hormones start to work on the cells and glands in the vagina and neck of the womb. Before puberty most girls have very little discharge. After puberty what is normal for one girl will not be normal for another. Some of us produce a lot of discharge, while others produce very little. Throughout the month you will also notice it varies in colour, what it feels like, how sticky it is and how much of it there is. What is not normal is if the discharge becomes smelly or greenish in colour, or makes you itchy. All these may mean you have an infection, especially if you have put yourself at risk by having had sex without using a condom. Some discharge is normal, but if it doesn't seem right or you've had unprotected sex, get it checked out by a doctor or nurse.

Dear Dr Ann – Hi there this is really embarrassing. **I get lots of discharge, which is milky and can be quite watery or thick, and it really smells.** Though I have never used a tampon and am a virgin; is this normal?

Dear 'Heavy discharger' – It is very unlikely to be anything too serious and it is most probably just your hormones making the cells of your vagina wall very active and produce lots of secretions – some people produce a lot, others a little. Normal vaginal secretions can smell quite a bit, but if it is really smelly, it would be worth getting your doctor (or his/her nurse) to take a swab just in case there is some kind of infection. This can be easily treated, so don't be embarrassed.

ABOUT CLITORISES AND HYMENS

Dear Dr Ann – **Could u please tell me what a clitoris is because my boyfriend wants to know?**

Dear 'Clitoris wonderer' – Your clitoris is an extremely sensitive bit of your body, the 'head' of which you can see just in front of your urethra (the hole you pee out of) and most of which is normally covered by your labia (folds of skin each side of your vagina). It is the equivalent in girls of a man's penis and gets hard when you feel sexually excited (the equivalent of when a man gets an erection). But most of the 'shaft' of your clitoris is hidden. During sex, the shaft and head get swollen because the blood supply to them increases – and the head of your clitoris becomes even more sensitive.

In girls the entrance to the vagina is covered by a very, very thin skin called the 'hymen'. There are little holes in it, which allow vaginal and menstrual discharge to get through. The common meaning of being a 'virgin' is that you have not had sexual intercourse and therefore this layer of skin is still there. The 'hymen' often tears naturally during sporting activities or when you insert a tampon. This does not mean that you are not a virgin.

Dear Dr Ann – I'm 17 and have a very loving boyfriend. We're ready to have sex and are both virgins. I've read in a magazine that **i'll bleed when my hymen tears** when I lose my virginity. is this true and if so how much am i likely to bleed?

Dear 'About to lose it' – It sounds as if you have thought carefully about this – which is great. To answer your question – most girls do bleed when they first have intercourse because the hymen gets torn, but the amount can vary greatly. This can vary from the odd drop of blood to soaking a couple of sanitary towels. It's really never bad enough to need to see a doctor. If you have been using tampons, it is less likely to be so bad. And don't forget to use contraception!

⁂4 BEST BREAST FACTS

Breasts and nipples - all you need to know

Each girl's breasts are like her fingerprints – never the same as anyone else's. In most girls, they begin to grow at around the age of 10 through to 14 years. But there is huge variation – some girls' breasts start to grow before this, some start later. Research shows that breast growth can go on even into your 20s or 30s, though most of it takes place between 10 and 18 years of age.

Your nipples contain the endings of the milk ducts that release milk when you are breast-feeding. They vary in size from the size of a 10p piece up to 5 centimetres. Their colour can range from pale pink to dark brown, and they may have a few hairs attached to them.

● TOO BIG, TOO SMALL

Models in films, underwear adverts, magazines, music videos, etc., may appear to have 'super' breasts. But in fact their breasts have often been taped, surgically made bigger or smaller, digitally altered, pushed up, pushed down, pushed out, pushed in – all in the name of artificial perfection...So don't be taken in.

Dear Dr Ann – **I have tiny boobs!** I don't really even have boobs, just huge nipples! And they stick in instead of out – is there something wrong with me?

Dear 'Person with tiny boobs' – There's nothing wrong with you. Women's breasts tend to grow with time anyhow. If you look at the majority of models, they tend to have small boobs and relatively large nipples. The fact that your nipples are large means that your hormones are working OK. Be patient, and even if your boobs don't grow to be huge, be happy with the end result – because that's the way that you are.

Dear Dr Ann – **I am almost 15 years old and my body is so messed up!** I am a very normal weight, have plenty of hair in the right places and I have been having my period off and on for about 6 months or so now (depending on if I am playing a lot of soccer or not). But I hardly have any boobs at all (I can barely even fit into an AA!) and they haven't grown since I was 11 or 12! What is going on with my body??? PLEEEEASE tell me that I won't be stuck in a less-than-AA for the rest of my life!!!

Dear 'Worried about being AA-size bra' – I'm afraid I can't predict whether you are going to have small breasts for the rest of your life. It doesn't sound as though your body is messed up at all – just one kind of normal. People with smaller breasts are just as beautiful and attractive as people with bigger breasts. And if you're worrying about boys – it's what you're like yourself that matters to them, not the size of your breasts.

Dear Dr Ann – **My breasts are currently very small** and my friends are telling me that it is because i only wear sports bras. Is it true? Does the sports bra stop growth of the breasts? Some of my sports bras are quite tight-fitting, so does it affect the growth? Female age 14.

Dear 'Do tight bras stop breasts growing' – Sometimes friends tell you things that are wrong and

make you worry unnecessarily. Sports bras do not stop breasts growing and you probably have small breasts because that is the way you are made. You are only 14, though, so there is still time for them to grow bigger. You could check that the bra you wear doesn't make your breasts feel too squashed, though.

Dear Dr Ann – **Is there any way to make my breasts smaller?** I haven't got breasts, I've got a pair of basketballs strapped to my chest. I need steel girders in my bra to keep them safe. Girl age 15.

Dear 'Basketball carrier' – Many girls feel that their breasts are too big. They may be comparing themselves with their friends whose breasts may not yet be fully developed, or they may just not be used to the change in their body shape. Give yourself time to adjust to your new shape and make sure you get a really good, supportive bra. It is possible to have an operation to make your breasts smaller – if they are causing severe discomfort – but don't consider this until you are older.

Dear Dr Ann – **How much do you think breast implants cost?**

Dear 'Breast implanter' – About £3000, but don't even think about it. As all surveys have shown, boys/men really, really do like women with both small and large breasts. Unless there is a very, very good medical reason – like having had one breast removed, or one breast being very much smaller than the other – just don't even BEGIN to think of it. Doctors won't even consider operating on girls under the age of 18 unless there are extremely good medical reasons.

● ONE BIG, ONE SMALL

Each of your breasts will be a slightly different size from the other, just as one of your hands or one of your feet may be slightly bigger or smaller than the other.

Dear Dr Ann – **Hi, I'm 13 yrs old and one of my breasts is a cup 'C' and the other is an 'A'.** I can't find a bra that fits. I have to use tissue. Is this normal?? Help, it is really embarrassing!

Dear 'Perfectly normal' – No problems here. Many girls find that for some reason or other one breast develops faster than the other, and in the long run they roughly even up. Until they even out, why not pad your bra slightly? Occasionally one breast remains noticeably bigger than the other. Most people learn to live with this, but if it is a real problem, surgery is a possibility. But don't rush into this as most breasts even out by your late teens.

● BREAST LUMPS AND BREAST CANCER

Girls get breast lumps for a number of different reasons, but breast cancer in young girls is incredibly rare.

Dear Dr Ann – **I'm 14 and I've recently found a really small hard lump next to my left nipple.** It isn't sore to touch but it's really getting me down. I haven't told my mum because she doesn't really have the time to talk and it's quite embarrassing for me. Could you please tell me what this lump could be, and is it possible I have breast cancer? Please help!!!

Dear 'Breast lump worrier' – It is very, very rare in women of your age to have breast cancer – OK? You are just too young. The commonest thing is that girls get lumps before their period that disappear when they get their periods. This is because your period hormones stimulate the normal breast glands. In someone your age, breast lumps that do not go away after your period are most often caused by a fibroadenoma, which is a bit of breast tissue that has become separated from the rest of your breast tissue. Most of these disappear on their own, one in 20 get bigger, the rest stay the same size. And you don't have to do anything about them. The other thing that your lump could be is a small cyst containing fluid. If you continue to worry about it and it stays there, go and get it checked by a doctor.

Dear Dr Ann – **How do you know when you have breast cancer?**

Dear 'Wanting to know about breast cancer' – Almost all breast cancer occurs in women over 40 years old, and it is very, very, very rare in women under 20. The commonest way of finding breast cancer is because you discover a lump in your breast. But most lumps in breasts are not cancerous; however, they should be checked by a doctor.

● SPOTS ON OR BETWEEN BREASTS

Dear Dr Ann – **Is it normal to have spots in between your breasts?**

Dear 'Spotty cleavage' – It is quite common to get a rash under or between your breasts. They can be due to acne, like most young people get on the face or back at some time or another. The spots/rash can be caused by a yeast infection, as the yeast likes the warm, moist skin in this area. Some anti-fungal cream from the chemist should clear them up. Spots here can also be caused by a bacterial infection, which will need to be treated with antibiotics.

• NIPPLES

Nipples may stick out, be flat or even be inverted, where the centre of the nipple sticks inwards...all perfectly normally.

Dear Dr Ann – **i am worried about my nipples, as they are inverted.** i hate the way they look, and am worried that my b/f will too. i saw an ad in the back of a magazine, which said it had a cure. should i try this product? age: 15

Dear 'Person with inverted nipples' – You are worrying unnecessarily. There's no reason why your boyfriend should mind, and when it comes to having a baby and breast-feeding, they are likely to pop out. I'm not sure what is being claimed to be a cure, but always be wary of ads on the back of magazines making such claims – especially if they cost a lot!

• STRETCH MARKS ON BREASTS

About half of all women have stretch marks on their breasts. These white spidery marks happen naturally and are not caused by running without a bra, sleeping on your stomach, having too much sex...

Dear Dr Ann – **Just recently I've noticed fine red lines coming from my boobs.** I'm starting to worry that this may be a sign of some sort of disease, or is this normal?

Dear 'Worried about red lines on boobs' – Cease to worry. These are so-called 'stretch marks' and occur on about half or all women's breasts. The red tends to fade and become a whitish mark, and so becomes less noticeable. I'm afraid there is nothing that you can do about them – it is just the way that you (and lots of other people!) are made.

BOYS LOOKING AT GIRL'S TITS

Dear Dr Ann – **Why do boys always look at your tits?**

Dear 'Wonderer about tit-fancying boys' – The best way to find out the truth about this is to ask the boys themselves. But I guess it's because they find tits attractive and sexy. Research does seem to support what you say – though I'm sure they look at your face and other bits of your body too. You could also check out with your girlfriends which bits of a boy's body they look at.

Boys, when asked what size breasts they like best on girls, come up with a huge range of answers. Some like large breasts, some like medium-sized breasts, some like small breasts, but most of all they like the whole girl and her personality. After all, girls wouldn't normally choose a boy just from the size and shape of his willie!

 5 MASTURBATION RULES - OK?

A game for one or more players...

Masturbation means 'sexually stimulating oneself, or someone else, usually using your hands or fingers'. Masturbating someone else is also common when having sex – especially before people start to have sexual intercourse itself. Masturbation to orgasm is often part of so-called 'heavy petting'.

People masturbate because (a) it is easy; (b) it is enjoyable; (c) it is controllable by yourself and you can find out what you like sexually; (d) it helps relieve feelings of sexual tension; and (e) you do not get pregnant or get sexually transmitted diseases by doing it.

There is no special age when boys and girls normally start to masturbate. It can start as young as 6 years of age or less and many people go on masturbating over a whole lifetime. Masturbation is extremely common in young people because it is fun and harmless, but this does not mean you have to do it.

Boys usually masturbate by rubbing the skin of the erect penis up and down using their whole hand or just with their fingers so that the skin of the penis stimulates the underside of the end of the penis. There are no particular rights or wrongs about how often a person masturbates or whether you can do it too much. Some girls and boys masturbate several times a day, others once a week, once a month or less. What is important is that you feel comfortable about it.

Dear Dr Ann – **What happens if someone masturbates,** I am worried about my friend? I know he does it and he is only 13.

Dear 'Worried about friend masturbating' – Masturbating is simply sexually stimulating yourself or someone else, without actually having sexual intercourse. There is nothing, absolutely nothing wrong with it, and if there was a problem, just about everyone would have this problem because just about everyone masturbates. But there are no problems.

Dear *Dr Ann* – **I am 14 and I masturbate.** Every time I have an orgasm (or whatever the male equivalent is) I expect sperm to come shooting out like when peeing. But the only thing that happens is that I get a small bit of sperm at the tip and that is still very small. Also, the penis is supposed to flop down again but mine just stays stiff. HELP PLEASE!

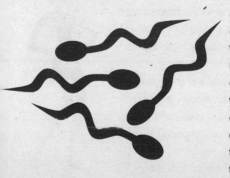

Dear 'Worried about very little coming out' – Doesn't sound as if there is anything wrong with you, and just to remind all masturbating 14-year-olds – masturbating is entirely normal. Two possibilities here are (1) you are not actually having a complete orgasm – a little bit of semen often comes out before you have the orgasm itself and the fact that you stay stiff might also indicate this. (2) Sperm does not always 'shoot' out during ejaculation, it quite often dribbles out. The amount that the average man ejaculates is only about a teaspoonful each time (and there is a considerable amount of variation from person to person). It is quite common for a man's penis to stay stiff for a while after he has 'come'.

Dear Dr Ann – **I think I masturbate too much** – up to 4 times a day and I am afraid that I am going to run out of sperm?

Dear '4 times a day' – This won't do you any harm at all, but aren't you boasting a bit? You may not have a lot of sperm to spare after three or four times, but leave it for 24 hours and you'll find it's back to normal – the usual teaspoonful. Your testicles work 24 hours a day, 7 days a week to make sperm – up to 30 million of them each time you ejaculate. You could populate all of France and Spain in one go.

However, what most boys do is to wipe the result with a tissue and throw it down the toilet. The only sign you're overdoing it is if masturbation interferes with your normal life – if everyone's out in the sun playing footie and you're skulking in the bedroom with FHM and doing it for the 19th time that day...and you're exhausted.

Dear Dr Ann – **Why do people sometimes use a picture of someone to masturbate over? Is it wrong?** Boy 16.

Dear 'Interested in masturbation' – It is entirely normal for both men and women – though it definitely seems to be much more common in men – to be turned on by sexual images. These are often pictures of nude men and women, as the human body is designed to be sexually attractive. It is also perfectly normal for both men and women to masturbate while reading about sex. Sexual images of people now occupy huge areas of the internet, and this is used by many people when masturbating. Whether much of this is 'good' or 'bad' depends on your moral attitude to sex. But what is NOT normal and is TOTALLY unacceptable is to use pictures of children being sexually abused or exploited or people being sexually degraded or subjected to violence.

Dear *Dr Ann* – **I am a 16 year old boy who, like most 16 year old boys, masturbates frequently.** The last few days, when i have been masturbating, i have been having to stop due to a severe headache which is caused by my masturbation. the pain is mainly concentrated towards the back of my head. Why is this happening?

Dear '16-year-old masturbator who gets headaches' – I'm afraid I don't know why you have started getting headaches when you masturbate. We do know that some people get headaches or a 'full feeling in their head' when they have an orgasm, but it isn't clear why. Try having a few days' rest and see whether you still get them. It does not sound like anything serious, although I can understand that it might have given you a fright. If it carries on, you should go to your doctor and have your blood pressure checked.

GIRLS MASTURBATING

Same or different, better or worse, more or less?
In girls the commonest way of masturbating is stimulating the clitoris with the hand or fingers. Many girls find that they enjoy the physical sensation of masturbating but not so much the psychological effects. Psychologically some girls see it as a 'lonely', 'self-absorbed' 'rather embarrassing', 'sad' activity. But other girls find that it gives them 'a sense of power', that it is 'liberating', 'gives them control.' Some have said that it is 'important because I don't have to be in a relationship to do it' and it 'taught me how to have an orgasm'. Other girls see it as 'a pure pleasure in itself'. On the whole girls tend to masturbate less than boys.

Dear *Dr Ann* – **i'm very worried, i'm a girl and i masturbated by myself** and now i'm not getting my period. could i be pregnant? could someone have masturbated somewhere and left sperm there and i touched it and it somehow got on my hands and when i stuck my fingers in my vagina could it have gotten in?? i'm going crazy, please help!

Dear 'Going crazy with worry' – No. From what you tell me you can't be pregnant, so don't worry. When periods start, they may be irregular. Most people masturbate, so don't worry about that either.

Dear *Dr Ann* – **Should a girl feel guilty about masturbating?**

Dear 'Girl who feels guilty about masturbating' – No, absolutely not. Almost everyone does it – some more often than others – and there is no specific amount that is right or wrong. What's right is just what you feel is right and what makes you happy.

Dear Dr Ann – **My friend asked me the other day if I masturbated.** I did not answer her and she made fun of me. What should I do? Girl 14.

Dear 'Person with a friend who asks awkward questions' – Don't feel embarrassed about whether you do or do not masturbate – because almost everyone does. Just tell your friend that it is none of her business.

So why all the secrecy?

Nowadays the majority of boys and many girls are happy to admit, without a second thought, that they masturbate regularly and are just glad of the pleasure that it gives them. But for some reason or other (probably because of the way people considered masturbation in the past) some boys and girls do feel 'guilty', 'dirty' or 'naughty' when they masturbate. THERE IS ABSOLUTELY NO NEED TO!

6 HOW NOT TO GET PREGNANT IF YOU DON'T WANT TO

All about contraception, pregnancy and abortion

Every year around 8000 teenagers in England and Wales under the age of 16 get pregnant. Half of these end up having an abortion. Most of these pregnancies could have been avoided in the first place if the couple had used contraception – or if the girl had taken the emergency contraceptive pill within three days of having the sex that got her pregnant.

WHAT ARE THE CHANCES OF GETTING PREGNANT?

Dear Dr Ann – **Could u become pregnant if u have unprotected sex** – if the boy gets his penis out before he ejaculates??

Dear 'Pregnancy worrier' – The answer is definitely and absolutely 'yes', and getting pregnant is not the only thing you should be worrying about with unprotected sex. Think of all those sexually transmitted beasties (like HIV, chlamydia, gonorrhoea, etc.) you are exposing yourself to. Most boys (and men) leak some 'cum' containing sperm, before they actually ejaculate. Also never, ever, believe a boy when he says that he can get out in time before he leaks or ejaculates – he CANNOT.

Dear Dr Ann – **Is it possible to get pregnant without having sex?**

Dear 'Person concerned about getting pregnant without sex' – Well, yes and no: it rather depends on your definition of 'sex'. If you mean 'can you get pregnant any other way than having sexual intercourse itself', the answer is 'yes'. If some sperm gets near a girl's vaginal opening, then there is a very small chance that one or more of the boy's sperm may climb up inside her and fertilize an egg. There is also 'artificial insemination', where a doctor uses a medical instrument to put sperm from a man directly into a woman's uterus via her vagina. This happens when a couple are having trouble getting pregnant.

Dear Dr Ann – I am 15 years old and me and my girl friend have had sex for our first time i really enjoyed it and so did she. We want to do it again sometime but we are **worried that she might get pregnant because the last time the condom split** but we didn't stop as we were really enjoying it. She did a pregnancy test after a week she wasn't pregnant – we were lucky but i was scared.

Dear 'Lucky escaper' – OK, but the first thing is that if this happens again, don't trust to luck but urgently get the emergency contraceptive pill (available from your local doctor or family planning clinic). Next thing to say is that if you are going to have sex and you want to make absolutely certain that she does not get pregnant, then she should go onto the pill as well as you using a condom. That way you can be absolutely sure. Remember that it is illegal for you to have sex with your girlfriend if she is aged less than 16 – you could be had up for 'unlawful sexual intercourse'. She could be prosecuted whether she is under 16 or not for having sex with you – which would be regarded in law as 'indecent assault'. When it comes to it, whether or not to prosecute depends on individual circumstances and on the best interests of the children involved. However, prosecution is much more likely if one or other of the people involved is being forced to have sex.

Condoms are the form of contraception mostly commonly used by young people. They not only protect you against pregnancy but also against sexually transmitted infections (STIs), including HIV. You can get them free from Young People's Clinics, family planning clinics and some GPs. You can buy them from chemists and in many toilets in public places, as well as from garages, newsagents and many other outlets.

The oral contraceptive pill is very good protection against pregnancy, but it is no good against STIs. The only thing that will protect you against STIs is a condom.

Dear Dr Ann — **If you have sex with a condom on can it bust?**

Dear 'Burst condom worrier' — They can burst and very occasionally do, but they test some of them (not the one you use!) by blowing them up with pints and pints of water. Usually it is not so much that they burst but they get nicked by a fingernail, or come off the end of a man's penis during sex. If this happens, then it is best if the girl goes to see her doctor for emergency contraception.

Dear Dr Ann — **I'm a 15 year old girl and I want to go on the pill.** I think my mom will put me on the pill but I don't know how to ask her. What am I supposed to say?

Dear '15-year-old who wants to go on the pill' — First you need to know that it is illegal for a boy to be having sex with you because you are under age. It is great that you want to talk to your mum about it. Why not just be up front with her and tell her what is happening? If you find that difficult, try writing her a note. Once you have told her, then you can both go off to the doctor's together to get the pill (which is free). And hopefully they will also give you some condoms for your boyfriend to wear, to stop any chance of you getting one of those nasty sexually transmitted diseases.

Dear Dr Ann – **i slept with a lad. i'm on the pill** (which i have been taking correctly). i just want to know if i need to be worried about being pregnant at all?

Dear 'Worried pill user' – It doesn't sound as though you need worry about getting pregnant if, as you say, you have been taking the pill correctly. Pregnancy when you are taking the pill is very, very rare – if you are taking it properly. But you do have to worry about sexually transmitted infections, such as chlamydia and gonorrhoea, which are not prevented by being on the pill. So next time use condoms as well.

Dear Dr Ann – **How safe is it to use the pill constantly without a break?** 16 female

Dear 'Can I use the pill without a break' – It is OK to take the pill constantly for a few months at a time. You won't have a period during that time. Doctors suggest that you take the pill continuously for 3 months, and then have a week off before starting it again. You won't be at increased risk of pregnancy during that week off, when you will have a period (but the period you get with the pill is not the same as your normal period). But if you take a longer break than a week off the pill, you will need to take other precautions to avoid getting pregnant.

● **HELP AM I PREGNANT?**

It is very risky having unprotected sex. Out of every three teenage girls who have unprotected sex, one will become pregnant.

Dear Dr Ann – **hi, my friend thinks she might be pregnant.** i was just wondering if she can get a free test from the doctors surgery? thanks

Dear 'Person with a friend who might be pregnant' – She will be able to get a free pregnancy test from her doctor's surgery or from another doctor's surgery, if she doesn't want to go to her usual

one for personal reasons. If your friend is worried about going to a doctor, she could go to a young person's clinic or to a family planning clinic, where they are also free (details on how to contact them are at the end of the book). If your friend does have a positive pregnancy test, she'll need to talk it over with someone she trusts and decide whether she wants to keep the baby or have an abortion. In either case she'll need to go and see a doctor.

Hey Dr Ann – **i'm a bit confused about when a girl can get pregnant.** in most magazines i read it says that you can get pregnant at any time, even when you are on your period, but in biology class at school we learned that you can only get pregnant on the 11th till the 16th day of a 28 day cycle. which is true?? and do the days change if your cycle is 25 days?? – Confused.

Dear 'Confused about when you can get pregnant' – You stand a much greater chance of getting pregnant 14 days before your next period, when your egg is released from your ovary . So if you have a 25-day cycle, then day 11 is the most likely one for you to get pregnant on. But the other things that you have to take into account is that sperm in the vagina can last for up to four days, and that the egg does not always get released precisely when it ought to. These two factors mean that there is some chance (but a lower one) of getting pregnant on almost any day of your cycle – especially if your periods are not absolutely regular.

Emergency contraception *should be taken within three days of having unprotected sex, but the sooner you take it, the more likely it is to work. Early on it works 98 times out of 100. You can get it free from your family doctor, another family doctor, a young person's clinic or a family planning clinic. It is also available over the counter from the chemist if you are over 16 – but then you usually have to pay for it.*

Dear Dr Ann – **if you get pregnant before the age of 16 can it stop you from having babies when you are older?**

> *Dear 'Worried about not being able to have babies'* – The answer is that having babies at any age is now extremely safe, and having a baby before the age of 16 won't stop you from having babies later – though it is better to wait. However, if you have unprotected sex without a condom at any age, then you have an increased chance of getting a sexually transmitted disease like chlamydia, which can block your fallopian tubes. These tubes lead from your ovaries, where the eggs are, to your uterus, where the fertilized egg needs to get to in order to become a baby.

Hi Dr Ann – Well, I feel silly, **but I always fantasize about being pregnant.** I'd LOVE a baby but I know I am too young. I'm just 14. Yet I love kids and walk around my room trying to pretend I am pregnant. What shall I do?

> *Dear 'Wanting to know what it would be like to be pregnant'* – This is not so unusual, but it is good that you know that you are too young to have one yourself at this stage. There are several feelings here. There is wanting to know whether all your bits and pieces are working OK – to know that you can have a baby. Most people don't have a problem getting pregnant – rather the opposite, most people have a problem trying NOT to get pregnant. Then maybe someone close to you has had a baby recently and you feel a bit jealous? Lastly, you may feel that you want to have a baby because it will be something special for you. Having a baby is wonderful if you wait till the right time. But when you are 14 is not the right time for you or a baby.

● ABORTION OR NOT?

In England, Scotland and Wales (but not Northern Ireland), it is legal for a woman to have an abortion before the 24th week of pregnancy – with the agreement of two doctors – if it is necessary for her mental or physical health. Most abortions are done as early as possible because it is safer for the mother. An excellent place to get further information about abortion is from a leaflet called 'Abortion: just so you know', available from the Family Planning Association (you'll find details of how to contact the FPA at the back of the book).

Dear Dr Ann – **what are the good/bad points of abortion?**

Dear 'Person interested in good and bad points about abortion' – The question of abortion raises strong feelings in people – both for and against it. Abortion is when a pregnancy is ended, either naturally by your body or by artificial means. What many people don't realize is that our bodies spontaneously abort up to four out of five pregnancies – very early on, so early that you may not even know that you are pregnant – usually because something is wrong with the unborn baby. Artificial abortion happens when a fertilized egg or embryo is removed from the womb, either by taking pills that makes your body reject the pregnancy or by removing the foetus by surgery. Legal abortion is very safe for the mother, and there is very little danger of not being able to have another baby in the future. See below for some of the 'arguments' about abortion – in the end, it is not really a question of 'good' or 'bad' points but rather about people's different moral views and feelings.

Views about artificial (induced) abortions – some common statements:

- *'women should have the right to choose so that every child is a wanted child'*
- *'the unborn child has a right to be born'*
- *'legal abortion saves lives because where abortion is illegal many women die as a result of having unsafe illegal abortions'*
- *'it is not that I think abortion is a good thing, but I don't think a woman who has got pregnant by accident should be forced to have a baby – it's not good for her and it's not good for the child'*
- *'why not have the baby and have it adopted, as there are lots of people waiting to adopt babies'*
- *'women don't become pregnant in order to have an abortion – it is always a difficult decision'*
- *'I'm really strongly against abortion because it is killing someone, but I might change my mind if I got pregnant by a mistake myself'*

Dear Dr Ann – **can you have an abortion on the NHS** if you are under 16 without your parents knowing?

> *Dear 'Person under 16'* – It is legal for a girl who is under 16 to have an abortion without her parents' knowledge. But the doctors she sees must feel that she fully understands what is involved and will try to get her to tell her parents. Remember, if you are in this position, you might think that your mum or dad would be very angry or even 'kill you' when you told them, but parents nearly always do offer help, love and support, even if they are not exactly pleased . So do tell them yourself or get a friend, doctor or nurse to tell them.

Dear Dr Ann – I am fifteen and **I am pregnant but no way am I going to have an abortion.** Please, please help me cos I don't know whether I should keep it.

> *Dear 'Pregnant person'* – This is a difficult decision to make at the age of 15 and you need to talk about it with someone you trust – maybe your mum, or someone else in your family. You will need to go to your doctor as soon as possible to get checked out and you may find him or her a good person to talk to. Another good person would be the midwife who will look after you during your pregnancy. As you are still at school, you should be able to get special help from a local teenage pregnancy adviser, who your doctor will be able to tell you about. If you are sure that abortion is not an option for you, then you will need to make another decision. You may want to keep the baby and look after it yourself, in which case you can get support and help in continuing your education. Your family doctor can provide you with details. Otherwise, if you want to have the baby adopted, you can contact the British Agencies for Adoption and Fostering (you'll find details at the end of the book).

BODY PIERCING – OUCH!

Ok, so you want to make a hole in it… but why?

Over thousands of years different cultures have chosen to 'pierce' every conceivable bit of their bodies. You name it, it's been pierced – noses, ears, tummy buttons, labia, penises, eyebrows have all had the treatment. Whatever turns you on, but the basic reason for it is 'body decoration' – to make people (as they see it) more attractive to one another.

A survey was recently carried out of 1003 young teenagers who had been 'pierced'. Most were aged between 11 and 18, and nearly three quarters were girls. This showed that, of those answering the questionnaire, 50% of boys and 84% of girls had had their ears pierced; 37% overall had had their belly button pierced; and 27% had had their nose pierced, 25% an eyebrow and 22% their lip. Around a quarter of the rest had had other bits of their body pierced, including their nipples.

● ## BELLY BUTTON PIERCING

Dear Dr Ann – **What are the dangers of getting your belly button pierced?**

Dear 'Thinking about belly button piercing' – The main danger in having your belly button pierced is getting an infection which goes all gooey, sticky and red – and it hurts. If it is done with a dirty needle, there are risks of getting the deadly

44

Aids virus or hepatitis. So make sure that if you do decide to have it done, you have it done by someone who is properly qualified to do it and uses sterilized needles and other gizmos.

Dear Dr Ann – **i got my belly button pierced on Saturday and it is still a bit red** do i need to go to a doctor i have cleaned it more that 2 times a day what shall i do girl age 16

Dear 'Pierced belly button' – Did it hurt to have it pierced? It sounds as though your belly button wasn't too keen to be pierced and is now a bit inflamed. It should settle down in a few days, but it would be a good idea to get some antiseptic like Savlon to help stop any infection. If it gets redder or starts getting more painful, you will need to see a doctor to get some antibiotic cream or pills. I hope you didn't do it yourself but went to someone who used a sterile needle. If not, please do get it checked out.

● THE 'OWS' AND THE 'OUCHS'

According to the survey, the commonest complication was pain, in around a third of those getting pierced, followed by infection (a quarter) and bleeding (a quarter). Ear-piercing was considered to be the most painful, followed by having one's belly button pierced. Boys were significantly more likely to experience these problems than girls.

Dear Dr Ann – **I'm going to get my tongue pierced, will it hurt?**

Dear 'Oral masochist' – Can't say I fancy the idea myself! I mean, how do you kiss properly with a knobbly thing there? Just remember – yes, it will hurt, it can get infected, and the metal stud can scrape the enamel off your teeth. If you do go ahead, find someone who does it properly and uses all sterile needles and other instruments. OUCH!

There are important rules to follow if you want to be pierced:

- *Only have piercing done by a reputable person with lots of experience and who uses prepacked sterilized instruments; otherwise you can get all sorts of nasty infections, including HIV and hepatitis.*
- *Make sure that whatever you are having 'put in' – rings, studs or other decorations – have also been sterilized.*
- *Watch out for local infections, usually occurring within the first few days, when whatever's been pierced can get red, sore and a bit pussy. Most of these will settle down with antiseptic cream from your local chemist.*

If this infection doesn't clear up within a few days or gets worse, check it out with a doctor, as you may need antibiotics, or to have your decorative 'object' removed.

8 HOW YOUR BODY GETS IT ALL GOING

The start of puberty

Puberty is the time when hormones in your brain tell your body to start getting the baby-making apparatus ready and working. For boys, puberty usually starts when you are between 10 and 13 years old and carries on till you are about 18. In girls, puberty usually starts earlier than boys – it can begin any time between 9 and 17 years, though commonest is around the age of 11.

● BOYS' PUBERTY – WHAT HAPPENS WHEN & WHERE

There's a lot of variation in the order in which things happen, but usually the first thing is that boys' balls get bigger. Next come pubic hair, hair under the arms and facial hair, followed by chest hair (not everyone gets this). You begin to grow taller, your muscles bigger, and your shoulders broader. Your voice starts to break and your penis grows longer and fatter.

Dear Dr Ann – **I'm 15, male, and I have pubic hair, but as yet no underarm hair, and I haven't started shaving** even though most of my mates have. My 13 year old brother has some underarm hair even though I don't, and my mates are starting to laugh at me for not having any, and it gets really tricky sometimes when my mates start talking about what razors they use or how often they shave. When should I start needing to shave?

Dear 'Non-shaver' – Sounds as if everything is well within the normal range. Usually what happens in puberty is, first, that your balls get bigger. Then pubic hair tends to come, followed by hair elsewhere – though there is quite a lot of variation as to what comes first. Over the whole of puberty your balls may get up to seven times bigger, and during the later stages of puberty your penis gets larger as well. But in general all these things start at different times in different boys, go on for different lengths of time and occur in a different order. In one way we all end up the same after we have been through puberty, but in another way we all end up different – because we all have different sizes, shapes, amounts of hair and so on.

Dear Dr Ann – **i've started puberty but most of my friends haven't.** am i different to my friends?? HELP!!!!! i'm a 11 years old and a boy.

Dear 'Pubic help seeker' – You may be different from your friends, but there is nothing abnormal about you. Fortunately we are all different from one another in lots of ways, and that also means everyone goes through puberty at different times and at different rates. It can happen any time between 8 and 16, but it normally happens to most boys and girls between 11 –14 years. In boys your hormones begin to kick in at the start of puberty, and this sets off a 'growth spurt' of up to 10 cm a year. Your weight increases at the same time as your body gets broader and more muscular. Your balls get bigger, your penis gets larger, and hair starts to sprout out in all sorts of places, including your chest, under your arms, around your penis and on your face. Your sweat glands begin to produce a different type of sweat, which is smellier, and also your voice gets deeper.

Dear Dr Ann – I am nearly sixteen, male and go to an all boys school. **I have not got anywhere near as far through puberty as most of my mates have.** I have some pubic hair around my willie, I am just starting to get some under my arms, and I still have a small penis, which is about 10 cm when erect.

Dear 'Puberty worrier' – You're normal and getting there. There is huge variation in when men start and finish puberty and you are well on the way. Patience, patience –10 cm is a good beginning!

Hi Dr Ann – I am worried because **people are all calling me gay and stuff coz my voice has not broken.** I'm NOT gay, why do they say this?? Help!

Dear 'Voice not broken yet' – For some reason people love teasing other people and don't realize how much it hurts. Ignore them and the teasing is likely to stop. I can guarantee your voice will break some time soon as you go through puberty. OK, so you are not gay, but gay men's voices break too!

● GIRLS' PUBERTY – WHAT HAPPENS WHEN & WHERE

Girls usually start to get breasts first and then get periods soon afterwards –though it can be several years later. Both are normal. Hair starts to grow around your genitals, then in the armpits and on the legs. The normal amount of vaginal discharge tends to increase.

Dear Dr Ann – i'm a girl 14 and 5'5" and **my breasts have started to grow a bit but I haven't got any hair down there** and all my mates have. When will it start?

Dear 'Girl with no pubic hair' – If you're 14 and that tall, then it shouldn't be long before your pubic hair starts to grow. It may seem like you haven't started puberty yet, but your breasts have started to grow and you have got taller. Your periods may start next. Often pubic hair doesn't grow till some way into puberty.

Dear Dr Ann – i am thirteen and a girl and **i don't have any signs of hair growing under my arms.**

Dear 'Hairless under the arms' – Don't worry, you are completely NORMAL. Hair growth in puberty starts at different ages in different people. Hair usually starts to grow in your 'pubic' area first, and a year or two later hair starts to grow under your arms. It can start to grow in some girls as young as 9 or it may not happen until you are as old as 15 or 16. If your pubic hair has started to grow, the hair under your arms will follow in the next couple of years. How much hair you get, how thick it is and its colour all vary from one person to another – it will also depend a bit on your race and colour generally.

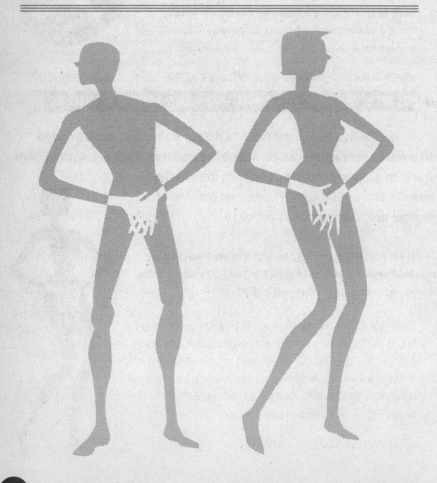

9 TOO HEAVY, TOO MANY, TOO FEW, OR HELP – NONE!

Periods – starting, stopping, coping

Boys may think themselves lucky because they don't have periods and girls may feel unlucky because they do. But boys and girls both need to know about them to avoid having babies when they don't want them and so they can have babies when they do want them.

Starting to have periods (known as menarche) occurs as part of puberty. A period is bleeding from a woman's vagina. Hormones produced in the brain cause a girl's ovaries to release one of the many thousands of eggs that have been sitting there since she was a baby. After this egg pops out, it passes along the fallopian tube to the womb (uterus), where a baby grows if the egg has been fertilized by a man's sperm. Every month the womb lining gets thick and ready just in case a fertilized egg becomes implanted and grows into a baby. If the egg is not fertilized, the microscopic egg and the womb lining all come away naturally as period blood.

The average age when periods start is 13.4 years. The time between each period is called the menstrual cycle. Although periods come approximately every month, only about 1 in 8 girls have periods that occur every 28 days exactly. Especially in the first year, periods may be far less frequent. It's as though the body is getting geared up and practising! Most periods last four or five days, but it is perfectly normal for periods to last anywhere between two and seven days, and the length may change from month to month.

Dear Dr Ann – **how do I know when my periods are going to start?** Girl aged 11.

Dear 'When will my periods start' – Some girls start having periods when they are only 8 years old, while others girls start as late as 16 or 17. Most start between 11 and 14 years. All this is completely normal – just like some girls are tall and others are short! It all depends on your hormones! The very first signs of puberty are that your breasts start to develop, and just before you start your first period, your breasts may become a bit sore. Some girls get a slightly whitish discharge on their pants before they get their periods, and this is an early sign that your hormones are beginning to work. It means that your period is likely to start in the next few months, so you need to be at the ready and carry a panty-liner with you. You can get a very good little leaflet called 'Periods – what you need to know' by sending a stamped addressed envelope to the Family Planning Association (contact details are at the end of the book).

Dr Ann – **Hi, I am 13 and I am really short but I haven't started my period.**

Dear 'Short 13-year-old with no periods yet' – Stop worrying, lots of girls don't start their periods till they are 15 or 16. It sounds like you haven't reached puberty yet and had your growth spurt. Periods will happen in their own time – and just think of all the money you are saving not having to buy sanitary towels or tampons.

Dear Dr Ann – **i'm scared i'll start my period at school,** i keep panty liners with me (just in case) because i had stabbing pains in my very lower stomach but I don't like the idea of asking the teacher to go to the toilet because they are locked until break and lunch. what shall i do?

Dear 'Period starting at school worrier' – Most girls worry that they will be 'caught short' and start their periods at an awkward moment, like at school or on the bus. Most people get a bit of warning. If you think that your period is about due and you don't know exactly when, why not wear a panty-liner anyhow and then you won't have any worries. It's wrong that your toilets at school are locked except at breaks and lunchtime. Try talking to the teachers or school nurse and tell them that locking the loos is just not on when you are 'on'.

Dear Dr Ann – **I thought I started my periods two months ago** but now they've stopped. Is this normal?

Dear 'Period stop-starter' – It's totally and utterly normal. Periods can take up to two years to settle down to a regular pattern. Until then you can skip a few months, and then get a really heavy one. Or you can get two in a month! Periods can also be late or skipped if you've been stressed or ill. But most women settle down to anything from 19 to 35 days from the start of one to the start of the next. If you keep a diary of when it starts, you should be able to predict the next one after a bit. Weirdly, though, girls often find they get in sync with their best girlfriends or family. Nobody quite knows why. It's something to do with pheromones – invisible scent chemicals that carry secret messages to your brain that you're not aware of.

● TAMPONS OR SANITARY TOWELS

Dear Dr Ann – **when i have my period the blood goes all over my knickers** because the pad doesn't stick. its really embarrassing as i feel wet and my mum always sorts through my washing and sees.

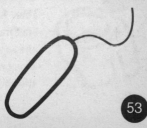

Dear 'Messy knickers' – Don't be embarrassed. Periods are messy and almost everyone gets messy yucky knickers with a period sometimes – including your mum, so I'm sure she won't mind at all. Try some different types of pads, ones that are slightly bigger perhaps and that stick better, or consider tampons, which fit inside your vagina and soak up your period blood before it leaves your vagina. Tampons come in different sizes, and it is a good idea to use 'mini' tampons when you start, as these are easier to insert, until you get used to them. Some tampons come with special inserters, and they all have a string attached to them, to make it easier to pull them out. You are still a 'virgin' if you use tampons. You will normally need to change a tampon or sanitary towel several times a day. Both tampons and sanitary towels come with detailed instructions on how to use them, as there are several different types of each.

Dear Ann – **i went swimming today when i was on** and tried to use a tampon for the first time! it really hurt when i put it in half way and so i had to not swim is there something wrong with me? from worrier

Dear 'Tampon worrier' – Girls often have trouble the first time they use a tampon, as it can take a bit of practice to get them in. First try using a thinner one, especially at the beginning or end of your period, when normally you will be losing less blood. If you are a bit dry, try wetting the tampon under the tap before using it. Very occasionally girls do have some problem with having a very thick hymen (the normally thin layer of skin covering your vaginal opening you are born with). This may need checking out. If you are having real trouble, you should think about just sticking with sanitary pads.

Dear Dr Ann – **Can you go to the toilet whilst you have a tampon in?**

Dear 'Worried about tampons and going to the loo' – The answer is definitely yes. It sounds like you may need to find out a bit more about your own anatomy! In brief –girls have three holes in the genital area. The one at the front is called the urethra and is for the urine (pee) to come out. The middle hole is the vagina. This is where the tampon is inserted and where the blood comes out during a period. The third hole, at the back, is the anus (your bum hole). Boys only have two holes – the urethra at the end of the penis, where the urine and sperm come out, and the anus, which is the same as in girls. Perhaps that is why you were confused.

● GETTING TO LOVE YOUR PERIODS

Women will have between 400 and 500 periods during their lifetime, so it is well worth getting used to having them. Still, some people will complain that they are too light, too heavy, too often, too few or too painful.

Dear Dr Ann – **I feel a complete mess in the couple of days before my period** – I can't stop crying, I bite everyones heads off, I hate myself and everything is totally out of perspective. Is there anything I can do – any remedies or websites you know about? thank you!

Dear 'Head biter' – Most girls feel at least a bit grumpy before their period starts, and this usually goes away once it has started. Keep a diary of when you feel like this and when your period starts, so that you know exactly when to expect it next time and realize that is only PMT, or premenstrual tension (or PMS – premenstrual syndrome). Then you can warn those around you. Next – taking exercise around this time is a good idea, because it releases the body's natural endorphins, which help your mood. Some people find Evening Oil of Primrose or Vitamin B6 help them – you can get them at your local chemist's. If it is still a problem, go and see your family doctor, because sometimes, if the PMT is very bad, taking the 'pill' can help. Try not to take yourself too seriously when you fly into a rage with your shoelaces and then burst into tears. It's not you, it's your hormones, and you'll soon be back to normal. Stay in and have a good sulk in front of the TV.

Dear Dr Ann – **I've started my periods and I wish I never had.** It really kills me for a few days, I get wicked tummy ache and I throw up, and it's like someone's jumping on my tummy or something. This isn't normal, what can I do?

Dear 'Person with someone jumping on your tummy' – Getting cramps before your period happens to a lot of women. It's a sign that your uterus (womb) is healthy, squeezing the lining out so it can grow a new one. But yes – it can feel like your stomach has just done five rounds with Lennox Lewis. Well, there are a couple of things you can do to ease it. Try lying down with a hot-water bottle and taking some painkillers like Paracetamol or Ibuprofen (remember to check the packet for the correct dose). If your life really comes to a stop once a month, your doctor can prescribe something stronger. Taking exercise often helps period pains.

Dear Dr Ann – **I have very heavy periods and they stop me doing stuff.** I only started about 8 months ago and am still not used 2 them. My periods can last almost 8 days instead of 5, and the 1st 3 days are horrible. Sometimes I am changing (normal flow) pads every hour. Am always worrying about leaking especially when out/at school. what can i do?

Dear 'Worried about heavy periods' – You should stop worrying and get some help. The amount of blood you lose during each period varies but is on average around 30 mls (6–8 teaspoonfuls), but it is mixed in with a lot of other gunk so may seem like a lot more. There are several different medicines available, which your doctor can prescribe and which will make your periods lighter. These include mefenamic acid, tranexamic acid and sometimes the oral contraceptive pill. In the meantime try using some more absorbent pads. Don't stop doing stuff because of your periods – rather get some help to get them sorted.

● IRREGULAR, MISSING AND LATE PERIODS

Dear Dr Ann – I don't know what my problem is. **I can never seem to get the dates right on my period.** I always end up with bloody underwear at the start of my period. I've had to throw away a lot of knickers and I'm wondering how I can plan right. Also my period sometimes comes early and sometimes comes late. Is my body messed up? – From Worried age 12.

Dear 'Worried about body being messed up' – No need to worry, your body is not messed up – just sorting itself out and the hormones getting into some sort of regular rhythm. Periods often take time to get regular, and in some women they are always a bit irregular. Keep a diary of when you get your period, which will help you work out a pattern. Always have some panty-liners with you, which should help with the knickers problem, as will some special stain remover.

Dear Dr Ann – **does 'not eating properly' affect how regular your period is?**

Dear 'Not eating properly and periods' – Yes, eating problems can affect your periods. Girls with anorexia usually stop having periods when they lose a lot of weight, and their periods only start again when they start eating properly and put on weight. Girls with bulimia also tend to have irregular periods.

Dear Dr Ann – **i am 2 weeks late on my period** – i think i might be pregnant but i used a condom.

Dear 'Worried about being pregnant' – If you used a condom correctly, then the chances that you are pregnant are small. But this doesn't mean that you shouldn't get checked out – just in case! The best thing is to get a 'do it yourself' pregnancy test from the chemist – the instructions on the box make it clear what you have to do. Alternatively you can get a free test from your doctor, your local family planning clinic, or young person's clinic. If you are pregnant, get advice quick – whether you want to keep the baby or not.

Common reasons for missing or stopping periods in teenage girls include:

- *losing weight because of anorexia or other eating problems*
- *taking lots and lots of exercise, such as running a marathon*
- *lots of travel*
- *There are other reasons, which are not clear, but the most common reason is pregnancy. So if you miss a period or your period is late and you could have got pregnant, always go and get a pregnancy test to check it out.*

10 HATING YOURSELF, THE WORLD AND EVERYTHING IN IT

Moodiness and depression

We all get moody, fed up, feelings of being left out, stressed and anxious sometimes, so you are probably no exception! But what is bad is when these feelings get so overwhelming that it stops you from doing anything well and makes you feel totally hopeless. When things do get too much for you, you may become grumpy, lose your sense of humour (assuming you had one in the first place!), feel tired all the time, find it difficult to get to sleep, go off your food or overeat, or get very jumpy. You may have difficulty concentrating and be unable to make decisions. If you are very, very anxious, then you may get sweaty hands or butterflies in your tummy. And you may feel hot and cold, want to pee all the time, feel that you are going to crap in your pants, feel sick, and feel your heart beating harder and faster.

● FEELING FED UP AND MOODY?

Dear Dr Ann – **I woke up in a horrible mood and everything made me cry.** My mom spoke to me and then I started to cry and my mom said we all get this sometimes. What does she mean? Female age 14.

Dear 'Girl in a horrible mood' – Your mum is right that we all get sad and moody sometimes and feel like crying. It may

58

even be difficult to work out why you are feeling so sad, though sometimes it is because something horrid has happened or you are worrying about something. Sometimes, when you feel like this and someone is nice and sympathetic, like your mum has been, it makes you feel able to cry and crying can make you feel better. Talking to your mum about your moods may also help you try and find out why they are happening. If these moods are happening a lot, try keeping a diary of when they happen to see if they are linked to your periods (if you've started them?) and therefore linked to the hormone changes that happen in your body each month. This is sometimes called PMT (premenstrual tension). If these moods are very frequent, it may mean you are depressed and you should go and talk to your doctor.

Dear Dr Ann – **I feel angry all the time** for no reason, girl age 12.

Dear 'Angry for no reason' – You may be right that there is no reason for you feeling angry, but it also may be that you just cannot see what the reason is yet. Young people often have mood changes around the time of puberty and can't pinpoint what it is all about. Keep a diary of your angry feelings to see if they do  relate to periods or anything else going on in your life. Also it might help to make a list of the things that make you happy and the things that make you angry, to see if you can get any clues. Making sure you do regular exercise may also help get rid of some of those angry feelings

---

Dear Dr Ann – it's not a major problem but at the moment i hate life. **i've just started sixth form in another school and i hate it.** the subjects are ok and the teachers seem pretty nice but i haven't settled in at all. i've been there just over two weeks and i haven't made any friends at all. the majority of them know each other really well and they have already got their groups of friends and they don't want any more. i feel really left out. all i want is a friend.

Dear 'New sixth form hater' – It is always difficult moving into a new group, especially when everyone else seems to know each other. The problem is that the other sixth formers may be completely unaware of how you are feeling, as they may never have been in the same situation. You will have to be patient, but try taking part in activities like sport and after-school clubs. Also grit your teeth and try and be friendly with anyone you like the look of – we all feel isolated, shy and embarrassed at times, but also we may not realize that other people feel the same way! If you are feeling down yourself, everyone else appears super-confident. But they aren't really, it is just an appearance – so keep trying.

Dear Dr Ann – **I have been feeling very lethargic recently** and find getting up in the morning difficult. I have been on anti-depressants every day after feeling down, but feel that I don't need them anymore. Would this be causing me to feel tired all the time?

Dear 'Feeling tired all the time' – These feelings of lethargy happen to many of us as a natural and normal part of life. But yes, it could be that you are still depressed, and yes, it could be the anti-depressants. Or it could just be that you are going to bed too late. It is definitely worth checking things out with the doctor who started you on anti-depressants, to find out whether you need to go on taking them or if you should change to another kind.

If you get moody, stressed and anxious, what can you do about it?

- Talk to your mum, dad or a friend about your anxieties, as sharing them with other people often helps.
- Make a list of all the things that are making you moody, stressed and anxious and think about what you might do about each of them individually, as problems looked at one at a time are easier to deal with than a vast great lump of problems.
- Take some exercise – run, jump, swim – it doesn't matter what, as all forms of exercise help produce 'endorphins' in your body, which make you feel good rather than anxious.
- Give yourself a break and do something that you really enjoy.
- Try changing the way that you think about your life. Instead of thinking 'I am a failure; no one loves me; I can't do my homework; everyone else is better than me', try thinking: 'There are things that I can do well; I've actually got some good friends; there is some homework that I can do OK; there are some things that I am better at than other people.

FEELING LIKE HARMING YOURSELF?

People often feel like harming themselves to relieve a feeling of unbearable tension. One way of harming, which is especially common in girls (but also happens in boys), is called 'cutting'. This is where you feel you've got to scratch or cut your arms with scissors, knifes, razor blades or pins. Girls who cut themselves describe an overwhelming feeling of anger and frustration, and they say that cutting themselves somehow lets out this anger and frustration. People who cut themselves seem to find it hard to express their feelings in other ways, and cutting certainly has the effect of drawing attention to yourself!

Dear Dr Ann – **I am in foster care and I cut my body** in temper to release my stress – can you give me some advice? Asked by: Stressed in Foster Care.

Dear 'Stressed in foster care' – I am so sorry to hear about your troubles. You haven't said why you have had to go into foster care, but are there things upsetting you where you are? Do please try and find an adult that you can trust and talk to about the way that you feel and what is happening – a teacher, a doctor, the school nurse, a good friend, a relative? If none of these are available, what about phoning the Childline and talking to them? Their number is 0800 1111. It is quite common for young people, especially girls, to cut themselves to release tension. It usually means that they have difficulty expressing how they feel in other ways, but if you can talk to someone about it, that could make all the difference.

Dear Dr Ann – **I'm 18 and I've been self harming myself for 2 years now.** I dont think i'll ever be able to stop. my arms are a mess of scars and i dont see the point in stopping if my arms couldnt really get any worse. i know i need to stop mentally though. I've been put on anti-depressants, they made me feel worse with a false sense of emotional stability. All i can think about is dying all the time and if i wasn't so scared of doing it then i would kill myself. Please help me before its too late.

Dear 'Person who is self-harming' – It sounds as if you are quite seriously depressed and should get some more help URGENTLY. Just because one

61

anti-depressant hasn't helped you doesn't mean there are not others that WILL help. You may feel desperate now, but with the right kind of help and time, things are likely to get better – so do not despair. There are some very practical things you can do when you feel bad about yourself. Make a list of your main worries, and work out and write down for each one what you think will help. When you feel you want to harm yourself, try having a list of distractions like talking to a friend, going for a walk or making yourself something to eat. Have a special 15-minute worry time during the day, which is when you can gather all your worries together, and at the end of 15 minutes mentally throw them away. Running, swimming, exercise in general helps because it releases a chemical called endorphin, which is a natural anti-depressant.

● R U DEPRESSED?

There are two main sorts of depression. First there is depression coming from feelings caused by things that have come from outside you – like worrying that your parents are splitting up, being ill for ages, or failing your exams. This kind of depression is painful, but is also entirely normal. Then there is depression that seems to come from inside you, when you can't stop having feelings like 'I'm lonely – no one likes me', 'I just can't face the outside world', 'Nobody loves me', 'What's it all for anyway?', 'I'm a loser – why bother?', 'My life is a mess', 'Why am I so crap?'. This second kind of depression is when something collapses inside yourself. Gloom and greyness descend on everything in your life for no obvious reason.

Dear Dr Ann – I need help. I'm fed up. I don't know what is wrong with me but I wish I did. **For days now I have just felt totally done in, not wanting to do anything,** can't be bothered with my friends – nothing interests me, everyone is getting at me.

Dear 'Totally done in' – Sounds to me like you're more than fed up, maybe you're a bit depressed. Being depressed is a real medical illness that affects your mind, even though it feels as if your body has given up too. It hangs around and colours all your feelings black. Being fed up is a feeling that comes and goes. Most people get fed up and even a bit depressed at some point in their lives – even doctors! But for some depressed people, depression takes over their whole life. Things to ask yourself are (1) do you feel tired all the time? (2) do you feel fed up all the time?

(3) do you feel that everything in the future is going to be bad? (4) do you feel no confidence in yourself? (5) do you find it hard to go to sleep and that you are waking up early? (6) do you find it impossible to talk to your family and friends about this? (7) do you find it hard to make up your mind? (8) do you find yourself crying or feeling sad for no good reason? If some or most of these are true, you've got to try talking to someone about how you feel – your mum or dad would be a good starting point. Perhaps if you can't talk to them, that's one of the things that makes you depressed. Or are there other family people you can talk to? Or a teacher or your family doctor?

Dear Dr Ann – **i've been seeing a counsellor and psychiatrist due to my depression.** they haven't given me any pills or anything. what can i do to let them know how bad i feel, i need help – i just don't seem to be getting better.

Dear 'Person with depression' – Seems like you need to talk some more with your counsellor and psychiatrist, but if you are having difficulty explaining how you feel, try writing them a letter. But remember, many people with depression do get better without pills, just by being able to talk to someone about how they feel.

● WHEN YOU FEEL LIKE ENDING IT ALL

Almost everyone has suicidal thoughts, when you feel that life is not worth living. For most of us these are fleeting, one-off moments. But if you're depressed, thoughts like these come back again and again, and make the depression worse. It will help to talk to someone close to you

about these feelings, but it can also help to talk to someone you don't know personally – like the Samaritans. Their website is at www.samaritans.org, where you can send an email about how you feel, and they'll reply within 24 hours. Or you can call them on 08457 909090.

Dear Dr Ann – **I am a 12 year old girl who is very depressed. I have thought of suicide** but I don't know. Please help!!!

Dear 'Very depressed' – I am so sorry. Actually feelings of depression and thoughts about suicide happen in lots of young people, so you are not alone. The trouble is that parents and other grown-ups sometimes don't realize this and think that you are just being 'difficult' or 'sulky'. Try talking to your parents or your friends about the way that you feel. You could also try keeping a diary and writing down how you feel – this often helps, perhaps because it helps put things outside yourself. Being depressed is just like being ill in other ways, like having pneumonia or bad periods, and if that were the problem, you would tell other people about it, wouldn't you? The main thing is that there are ways of helping. And you must go to see your family doctor and talk to her or him. If this is too difficult, ring the 'Samaritans' and talk to them.

Dear Dr Ann – i feel really low and i'm having trouble with my parents. **I really feel like killing myself** and my boyfriend is the only person stopping me. i've talked to my doc and he said i've just got to shut up and put up with it. PLEASE HELP ME!!

Dear 'Person thinking of killing yourself' – I am really, really sorry that you feel so bad about life – especially if it is your parents who are the trouble. Great that your boyfriend is so supportive – keep talking to him. Why not also try writing down the way that you feel? If you can't show this to your parents, then show it to a family friend or a teacher who you like, and discuss it with them. I am also really sorry that your doctor is so unhelpful. You can ask to see another doctor in the practice or change to another practice. Please, please don't give up trying to find help, though.

Dear Dr Ann – **i am worried about my friend. she has taken an overdose** before and had to be rushed to hospital and today she showed me where she had tried to cut her wrists. i don't know what i should do whether i should tell someone or just keep it to myself. i am so scared that she tries something stupid like this again please help me 14 year old female.

Dear 'Worried about a friend who has taken an overdose' – Sometimes you have to tell someone else about something you've been told, even if the other person wanted you to keep it a secret. This is one of those times. It sounds like your friend needs help from a doctor. Don't feel you alone have to sort it out or give her all the support she is going to need. Talk to your mum, the school nurse, a teacher or another adult you trust. Your friend may be cross at first, but she probably told you because what she really wanted was some help.

11 HAIR HERE

AND NO HAIR THERE

Too little hair where you want it, too much where you don't

'Macho man' is happy to have almost as much hair as a your average gorilla before he is likely to complain that it is a problem, whereas most girls may feel threatened by the faintest shadow of hairiness. We all have hair (both males and females) on our bodies, but some have more than others. Obviously the darker your body hair and the lighter your skin, the more noticeable the hair is. Also certain ethnic groups have more hair than others. The only place that people never normally have hair is on the palms of their hands and the soles of their feet. Otherwise there are hair follicles all over your body, even if the hairs in some places are extremely fine.

● UNWANTED HAIR, AND HOW TO GET RID OF IT

Dear Dr Ann – **what do you do about unwanted hair on your body and face?** Anon female.

Dear 'Female person with unwanted hair' – Some people learn to live with their body hair and others, like yourself, may want to get rid of it, or at least some bits of it. Hair on legs can be got rid of by shaving – but watch out not to cut yourself! Waxing packs are good and you can get them from the chemist, or you can have a wax treatment at a beauty salon. Waxing hurts more than shaving, though the effect lasts longer. Your leg hair will tend to grow back in 4 to 6 weeks. If you have facial hair, don't start shaving or you may begin to look a bit stubbly. But you can pluck them out, use a special face cream or have facial electrolysis at a reputable beauty salon (though they may not do it if you are very young). Laser treatment can also be used to get rid of unwanted hair. If you have suddenly become very hairy and no one else in your family is, then best check with your doctor to make sure that you don't have any hormone trouble.

Dear Dr Ann – **Please help me, I have dark hairs all over my stomach,** how can I get rid of them? I haven't tried shaving or creams because I don't want to be left with hair stubs. This is really getting me down, please tell me how to get rid of them? Female age 15.

Dear 'Dark hairs on stomach' – All of us have hair on our bodies, just like all other mammals. There is also a huge amount of variation between people as to how much hair they have on different parts of their body. For instance, some boys have

very hairy chests and others have no hair at all, and they just have to learn to live with that. Please don't get down about it – and please don't try shaving it, as it will only grow back. If you worry about the hair on your stomach when you are swimming, find yourself a really sexy one-piece that covers them up. If there are only a few hairs, you could try waxing them off. If there are lots and lots – and on other parts of your body as well – then do get checked out by your doctor as it just may be some hormone imbalance.

Dear Dr Ann – **I have a really nasty mole with a black hair** coming out of it on my cheek. My mum says I should leave it alone or it will go bad. Boy age 14.

Dear 'Hairy mole worrier' – Be reassured: it's not dangerous to pluck hairs from moles and hairy moles are very, very unlikely to be cancerous. So do pluck the hair out or cut it off carefully.

Dear Dr Ann – **I'm really worried about shaving my legs.**
I've been doing it now for about a year, with an electric
razor. It takes me ages and ages, about an hour. I don't
know whether I'm just being a perfectionist or whether it's
my razor. Is it better to use a non-electric one? Girl age 14.

Dear 'Leg shaver' – There's no best way to get rid of the hairs on your legs.
Shaving your legs can cause hairs to grow back more quickly than methods like
waxing, which removes hairs from the roots. You put the wax on your legs and then
use the strips of material in the pack to pull it off along with the hairs. Ouch – yes, it
does hurt a bit, but the hairless effect lasts longer than shaving. Shaving, and
especially plucking, probably do cause hairs to grow back thicker and darker, as
they stimulate the hair roots. However, care should be taken with waxing, as
removal of hairs from their roots can cause in-growing hairs or double hairs to grow.
Regular removal of hair can help prevent this.

● TOO LITTLE HAIR

Dear Dr Ann – **my chest is bald** and me mates all look like they have doormats on
theirs – when will I grow some hair? 15 year old male.

Dear 'Person with bald chest' – Some boys have lots of hair on their chest,
some have a few wisps, and some appear to have none at all – though in fact they
do have very fine hair. The amount of hair we have on our bodies – including men's
chests – seems to be determined mainly by our genes. Luckily, some girls fancy men
with lots of hair on their chest and others fancy them without obvious hair.
Personally I doubt whether having a hairy chest is a 'make or break' factor in any
relationship!

Dear Dr Ann – **I am 14 and don't have to shave yet.** I'm afraid that I'll
never have to and my dad teases me about it.

Dear 'Non-shaver' – Enjoy it while you can: once you have
started to shave, you are going to have to do it practically every day
for the rest of your life (unless you decide to grow a beard!). It's a
bit like girls wanting their periods to start and worrying that
they haven't yet. Then they do start and it is a 'bloody'
nuisance for years and years. OK, so shaving isn't as bad

as periods (that's my opinion!), but when your dad teases you about it, he's probably just trying to get you to be a bit less serious about it. Because like me, he knows that it will happen soon enough.

Dear Dr Ann – **my hair is dropping out,** what shall i do? 12 year old male.

Dear 'Hair dropping out' – I can imagine how worrying this must be. We all lose some hair, so it's really a matter of how much. There are many different reasons for hair falling out and baldness. The commonest reason is your genes – if you are a boy and your father went bald in his 20s, it might be the same for you. Increased shedding of hair can also happen after an illness or pregnancy. Sometimes hair loss can be due to things like anaemia (low iron levels) or other hormonal causes. Local patches of hair loss may be due to a skin disease causing scarring and damage to hair follicles, or they may be caused by a condition that tends to run in families called alopecia areata. You can cause patches of hair loss by constant twisting and rubbing of a particular area. This can even happen without you realizing it as you go to sleep. If there is hair on your pillow when you wake up in the morning, this may be the cause. You need to see a doctor about this.

12 BLITZ THOSE ZITS!

...and all those other skin problems

Skin is wonderful stuff that covers our whole body and seems to hold it all together. Continuously renewing itself, it is waterproof and protects us from too much sun. It contains glands to keep it slightly oily, and sweat glands in the skin help to control our body temperature. The average human adult skin weighs 3–4 kg and, if spread out, it would measure around 2 square metres (best not to try this out, though).

● ZITS AND PIMPLES

Every teenager will have at least one or two acne spots at any one time, and most will have considerably more. The cause of acne is increased grease production by the grease glands (sebaceous glands) in the skin. These glands are found mainly on your face, back and chest. The amount of grease produced is controlled by your sex hormones, which is why acne tends to occur at puberty and clears up by itself as you get older. You can't 'catch' acne from someone else.

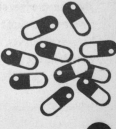

Dear Dr Ann – **I have visited my GP about my acne** he says that i have got moderate acne. I have tried one type of antibiotic and i was on them for about 7 months but they weren't working. I have been on some more now for about 3 months but my spots are becoming worse.

Dear 'Acne sufferer' – If the antibiotics that your doc gave you don't work, you should see him/her again to discuss other options. If you haven't tried them already, Retin A lotion or cream might help – your doctor can give you a prescription for these. However, if your acne is really bad, it might be that, in the long run, you need to see a skin specialist, who could prescribe a very strong treatment called 'Roaccutane' – but you only need this if the acne is very bad and doesn't clear with other things. About using 'washes' – different washes suit different people, so if you have found a wash that helps, keep using it.

Dear Dr Ann – **I am always...constantly...never ending... having pimples on my face** even though I wash my face each morning. At least tell me there is a way of lowering the number of pimples on my face plz.

Dear 'Pimply person' – Try going to your local chemist and getting one of the many acne creams or lotions that have benzyl peroxide in. They work by peeling off the superficial layers of the skin and unblocking blocked-up pores. If that doesn't work, you should probably see your doctor for some antibiotic lotions or tablets.

Dear Dr Ann – **If my zits don't go away I'm going to kill myself** cos I am going to see some girls. One of them is called Joanne and is sort of a mixture of Cameron Diaz and Britney Spears but unless she's crazy she won't touch me with zits like these – I'm a human custard pie. Boy aged 14.

Dear 'Human custard pie' – Don't do away with yourself, because doctors can give you stronger stuff to dry up the skin, antibiotics to get rid of bacteria, and in severe cases stuff to stop your body producing so much grease. You're not going to have acne forever, I promise. By the way, it's best not to squeeze your spots – especially not the red ones, because it just makes them worse. But if you can't resist, go for a blackhead, with clean fingers.

A bit of sun is good because it helps produce Vitamin D in our bodies. But too much sun damages your skin, making it look old before its time, and increases the risk of getting skin cancer later. Our skin colour is determined by the amount of a pigment called melanin in it – the darker the skin, the more melanin, and better the protection you get against the sun's rays. If you are not fortunate enough to have lots of melanin, then there are high-factor sun screens you can get from the chemist.

Help Dr Ann – **Every inch of me hurts, including unmentionable bits I got sunburnt** when I fell asleep on the balcony...ow ow ow. My skin feels like it's leaking nuclear radiation. I was trying to get a tan to make my bod look a bit less pasty and a bit more likely to pull a bloke. But now I'm ketchup coloured everywhere.

Dear 'Burnt bloke puller' – Ketchup-coloured everywhere? I hope this balcony wasn't in full view of the street! Do you have any areas of your skin that have blistered? Because if you have, don't burst them. The skin over the blisters will help stop infections. If you have very bad blisters, you'll need to see a doctor. If not, then cool baths, sponging with cold water, and covering yourself with 'after-sun' lotion or calamine lotion will make you feel a bit better while your body is healing itself. Take some paracetamol to help with the pain (remember to check the packet for the correct dose), because it will probably go on hurting for a couple of days. It will get better and better day by day, but there is more to come. Your skin will tend to get itchy and then will start to peel off. Next time, use some suntan lotion – best to start with at least factor 15. It is not a good idea to get badly burnt again, as it might permanently damage your skin. Next time, remember 'sit under a tree from 11 till 3; slap on a hat; slip on a shirt; slop on the cream'.

We have 3–4 million sweat glands on our body. On a normal day they produce around half a litre of sweat, but this can increase to 3–4 litres an hour if you get really hot.

Dear Dr Ann – **I have very sweaty feet.**

> *Dear 'Person with sweaty feet'* – We all sweat a bit, especially from our hands, feet, armpits and face. Like being tall or short, it varies from person to person. And when we sweat, some of us smell more than others. Smelly feet are often due to fungal infections between the toes, which are more likely to occur with people who sweat more. I'm afraid you need to wash your feet at least once or twice every day. Also, nylon socks and trainers are the worst things for sweaty feet – so buy cotton socks.

Dear Dr Ann – **I am male and have a very bad sweat problem** that can't be controlled by shop deodorants, i've tried roll-ons and sprays but nothing works – i'm too scared to go to the doctor, what should i do?

> *Dear 'Person with a sweat problem'* – This is fairly common. We all sweat different amounts, and how much our sweat smells also differs. First, the simple things... Certain materials make you sweat more, particularly artificial materials. So try and wear only pure cotton clothes. Make sure that you wash regularly to get rid of the sweat – bathing or showering twice a day helps. You say that you have tried all the normal anti-perspirants. The best ones for sweating contain a chemical called aluminium chloride hexahydrate. A particularly strong one that you can buy over the counter from the chemist is called 'Driclor'. If that doesn't work, you should overcome your embarrassment and go and see your doctor, because he/she will be able to help.

> Stretch marks are scars caused by stretching or shrinking of skin. Cellulite is a type of fat that causes dimpling of the overlying skin and causes a lumpy appearance. The tendency to develop both of these things seems to be inherited. You may not like the look of either stretch marks or cellulite, but they are NOT going to do you any harm. And don't spend any money on creams or other treatments, because they may do more harm than good and they won't make them go away.

Hi *Dr Ann* – This is really embarrassing. A few months ago i put a bit of weight on through depression (my mum was really ill and in hospital) and i've lost it now i'm back to normal but **i have gross stretch marks.** How do i get rid of them?

> *Dear 'Gross stretch marks'* – Unfortunately it is difficult to get rid of stretch marks, and the creams that claim to make them magically disappear don't usually work! So don't go spending a fortune on them. You get stretch marks because that is the way your skin is made. But the marks do tend to fade and become less noticeable with time.

Dr Ann – **I think that I have got cellulite on the top of my thighs** but I am not sure as the dimple effect is very faint at the moment. How do I know that it is cellulite for sure as it is making me quite worried and depressed?

> *Dear 'Worried about cellulite'* – 'Cellulite' is just a fancy name for fat, especially the rather lumpy form of fat that women tend to get on their hips and thighs. It forms pockets under your skin, and this is what causes the puckering of the skin. Some people have made a lot of money sucking out cellulite from under the skin, but this can be dangerous and may leave scars on the skin – so you shouldn't have it done. What you should be doing is taking regular exercise, eating less fatty foods, and keeping on the move.

● SCRATCH, SCRATCH, SCRATCH...

Eczema is an inflammation of the skin, which causes sore, itchy patches, especially on the inside of your elbows and behind your knees. It is not infectious, so you can't 'catch it' from other people – you can kiss someone with eczema as much as you or they want!

> *Dear Dr Ann* – **I suffer eczema on my face** and although it is not all that itchy it is quite red and dry. I always feel self-conscious about it and I wonder how long does it last for and how should I treat it?

> *Dear 'Eczema sufferer'* – The important thing is that you can make it better. The facts about eczema are: it usually runs in

families; it affects at least 10 in every 100 people; it tends to get better as you get older; it is an inflammation of the skin caused by a whole lot of factors, which include 'allergies' – it is more common in people who suffer from hayfever. In some cases, it may be a reaction to some chemical in a cosmetic; hair dye, jewellery, washing powder, and make-up can all cause it.

If your eczema is caused by an allergy, then it will tend to come and go depending on whether your skin has been in contact with the substance causing the allergy – so see if you get it when you have used cosmetics, certain washing powders, etc.... and then avoid using them. However, it is often difficult to know what causes it, and the best way of treating it is to stop your skin from getting too dry with moisturizers (the cheap ones are as good as the expensive ones). If that doesn't help, you may need to go to your doctor and get something containing 'steroids', but don't use strong steroids on your face, or for a long time, as they may seriously damage your skin. Some people find complementary treatments such as Chinese medicines can also help eczema, but make sure you get them from a properly trained person. Otherwise you may be given medicines that contain high doses of steroids without being told.

Itching is feeling the need to scratch your skin and can be caused by many different things, including dryness of the skin and skin infections. If you start to scratch, the itching only gets worse – so it's best not to start!

Help, Dr Ann – **I've got itchy feet** – itchy feet as in scaly itchy skin between my toes.

Dear 'Itchy feet' – Well, either you're turning into a dinosaur, or you've got athlete's foot. Athlete's foot happens when fungi that normally live on your feet (where they harmlessly munch away on your dead skin cells) find themselves in moist, warm conditions – like when people get wet feet and then put their socks on again. These fungi think it's paradise and multiply a gazillion times. Then you start tearing your shoes off trying to scratch. Nip down to your local chemist and buy some antifungal cream and powder. Or if you go to your doc, you can get a free prescription for them. Dust your feet with the powder and smear the cream between your toes. It'll soon go.

Dear Dr Ann – **I have a really itchy scalp which makes it flaky.** I think its dandruff but I do have eczema – could it be on my scalp as well?

Dear 'Itchy scalp' – Dandruff is by far the most common cause of an itchy scalp, but yes, you can get eczema on your scalp as well, or even a bit of eczema and dandruff combined. Head lice are the other thing that makes your scalp itch like hell – the skin of your scalp gets allergic to their shit! If it's dandruff, then try one of the many anti-dandruff shampoos, till you find one that works. If none of them works, your doctor can prescribe something stronger. If it's eczema (and it is not easy to tell the difference), your doctor can prescribe some special shampoo. If it's lice, ask your chemist for the appropriate lotion and start combing your hair with a fine-toothed comb. This knocks the legs off the lice so they fall out of your hair.

Dear Dr Ann – **I feel lousy. I feel lousy cos I've got louses. I mean lice.** I'd reckoned I'd got lice cos my head itches like crazy and I have to scratch all the time

Dear 'Headlice owner' – Well, the first thing to do is to get someone to check your hair. If they can't see anything, get them to comb right through your hair with a special 'nit' comb, which you can get from the chemist, as you lean over a sheet of white paper. If you find little near-transparent beasties, a bit smaller than the head of a match, it's lice. Regular combing with a nit comb, or other very fine comb, helps anyway, because it breaks their lousy little legs so they fall off your head. But if you do have lice, you will need to go to the chemist's and buy some special anti-louse lotion. Please, please read the instructions carefully. And no need for embarrassment here, because lots of Posh heads (yes, probably even that one) have them. It's not your fault you've got them – they spread around when your head touches someone else's.

Dear Dr Ann – **My bum itches like mad.** What's wrong with me? From Scratchy.

> *Dear 'Scratchy'* – Sounds like you've got thread worms. They're very tiny and very
>  common – about 1 in 3 of the world's population have them, so
> you're not alone. And unlike a lot of other kinds of worms that
> people have in their guts, particularly in countries where people
> can't afford a good diet and decent hygiene, thread worms don't
> appear to do much harm other than give you an itchy bum. They
> get their name because they look like tiny white threads. They
> crawl out of your bum and lay eggs there, which is what gives you
> that crazy itch. What you need to do is nip to your local chemist
> and get some anti-worm medicine.

Dear Dr Ann – **I get all this itching around the top of my socks.** Scratch, scratch,
scratch, I can't stop myself. Mum says that they are flea bites, and there ain't nothing I
can do about 'em – is that right?

> *Listen 'Flea-bitten'* – Little fleas love the end of summer. I bet that you have a
> cat at home? The cat's fleas will have licked their lips at the sight of your legs, leapt
> on you, found the top of your socks (or around your belt – anywhere moist and
> cosy), and yum, yum – started tucking into you. Get down to your local
> vet and ask for some anti-flea stuff. Pop the cat into a string
> bag and spray her with whatever the vet gives you. She'll
> hate you for a few hours, but her fleas will be history.
> For your own bites – drop in at the chemist's on
> the way to the vet and get some cream with
> antihistamine in it. It will stop the itching.

Dear Dr Ann – **I got mosquito bites** on holiday in Spain. Other people seem to get a
small spot but mine are gross – they swell up into a large blister (like a burn),
and cause large open sores on my legs when they eventually burst. Is
there a vaccination of some kind that will prevent this on my next
holiday?

> *Dear 'Mosquito-bitten'* – Some people seem to be much more
> sensitive to insect bites than others and may get a very itchy bump.

There is no vaccination against them, but you obviously need to take maximum precautions, so here are some suggestions. Most mosquitoes bite at dawn and dusk, so keep yourself well covered during these periods. Use a mosquito net at night – they are cheap and easy to use. Put on lots of insect repellant – either sprayed on or as a cream. And if you do get bitten, use calamine or antihistamine cream.

● WARTY LUMPS

Warts can appear in all sorts of places, including hands, the soles of the feet (verrucas), willies and vaginal lips. They are caused by 'wart' viruses. These are infectious, so warts are normally picked up from someone else who already has them. Even if you don't do anything, most warts will disappear in a few months of their own accord, but others can be helped on their way! (To find out about warts on your penis or on your vaginal lips, see Chapter 1.)

Help, Dr Ann – I think I'm turning into a witch. **I've got warts.** Horrid knobbly lumpy warts on my fingers. I hate them, and I want to bite them off.

Dear 'Wart hater' – Please don't do that. I know they're horrid, but they're also infectious. If you bite them, the infectious virus that causes them and lives in the warty cells will spread more easily. By the way, the same virus causes the warts on your feet called verrucas. Now, there's a way to cure warts that often works like magic – better than any granny cure like pissing on your hands or using witch hazel. The magic remedy is called salicylic acid, which you can get from your local chemist. Just paint the stuff on, like nail varnish. It helps kill the warty cells. Then you have to scrape the dead skin off. It kills (on average) 75% of warts within three months, and the rest will eventually go away of their own accord. If they don't, then you can get them frozen off by your doctor.

Dear Dr Ann – Ouch, ouch, ouch – **my feet hurt when you press on the bottom of them and there are bumpy things there** – what are they?

Dear 'Bumpy feet' – Sounds like you may have verrucas, which are warts caused by a virus. They are like the ones you sometimes get on your hands, but because they are on the bottom of your feet, your weight squashes them inwards and makes them hurt. Ask your chemist for some verruca plasters. They're like little rings that stick to your skin around your verrucas. You put some salicylic acid inside each ring, and the stuff kills off the virus. You then have to scrape off some dead skin. Most verrucas will actually go away by themselves, whatever you do. But it may take some time – months or even years – and if they are hurting, it is worth doing something about them.

·13· YOU ARE WHAT YOU EAT

Eating, dieting and weight worries

What you need to eat to stay alive, grow normally and not get fat is probably less than you want to eat. What you need to eat is a mixture of different types of food, which are made of protein, fat and carbohydrates, as well as some essential minerals and vitamins. For instance, meats and cheeses both contain protein and fat, while fruits have carbohydrates and vitamins. Unfortunately, many foods contain much too much of some of these things and not enough of others. In the UK most of us eat a diet that contains too much fat, which is why so many people – including teenagers – are overweight. To see if you are eating right, you can try keeping a food diary for a few days. This way, you can find out what you are actually eating and check it against the foods suggested at the end of the chapter.

● **EATING TOO MUCH, TOO LITTLE OR JUST RIGHT?**

Dr Ann – **I am very overweight, what should I do?**

Dear 'Worried about being overweight' – You haven't said whether you are a girl or a boy, how old you are, how tall you are or what you weigh. I would need to know all those things to really tell you if you are overweight or not. The bad news is that

more and more young people are overweight – the good news is that you can do something about it. But dieting is NOT the answer: most people who go on strict diets end up stopping dieting, eating more than ever and getting even fatter. But you do need to change what you eat. Cut down on the fatty things – crisps, chips, cake, biscuits. There's no need to stop eating them altogether, but eat more fruit and vegetables – five portions a day. And start exercising – walk to school, ride a bike, go swimming – and watch less telly. I'm sure you've heard it all before! But soon you'll be less overweight.

Dear Dr Ann – **I eat all the time.** I'm not fat but i just love eating and i always eat sugary foods. If i'm thin now, will it catch up with me later?

Dear 'Food lover' – Unlikely, because you are probably doing enough to use up all the energy you get from the food you eat. If you keep up the exercise, then you keep burning up the calories. If you stop the exercise, then you may get fat – it's as simple as that. But remember, there are problems with eating too much sugar, especially if you're eating it all the time, because it causes your teeth to fall to pieces!

Dear Dr Ann – **My ribs stick out quite a lot and it is the one thing that i really don't like about my figure.** Is there any way to reduce this or build up more fat round my chest and not my belly? I know it's girls that are supposed to worry about their weight. Boy age 14.

Dear 'Sticking out ribs' – I get lots of questions from girls about how to lose weight, whereas boys are often worried that they are too thin. It really doesn't sound as though there is anything wrong with your shape, and it may be that all your family are the same. You will find that the muscles around your chest get bigger as you go through puberty and have more of a growth spurt. Whatever you do, DON'T try taking hormone pills to build up your muscles – they are dangerous and can harm your health. Just make sure you eat a healthy diet and do some regular exercise. Learn to love that thinner look – it's healthy! Thin, wiry boys are often good at sports that the musclemen can't do, like rock climbing and running.

Dear Dr Ann – **How many calories can i eat a day?**

Dear 'Wanting to know about calories' – Calories measure the amount of energy that is contained in different foods. We all need to eat enough food to get enough energy to do all the things we want to do, but the body itself also needs enough calories to work properly – even if we just lie in bed all day. The more active you are – like running or swimming or doing other exercise – the more calories you need to take in in your food. So I can't tell you the exact amount of calories you need, but the figures below will give you a guide.

Boys need...

aged 7–10 years	about 1970 calories a day
aged 11–14 years	about 2220 calories a day
aged 15–18 years	about 2755 calories a day

Girls need...

aged 7–10 years	about 1740 calories a day
aged 11–14 years	about 1845 calories a day
aged 15–18 years	about 2110 calories a day

Dear Dr Ann – **I am really worried about my weight,** every time I have something to eat I get paranoid that I am going to put on weight by eating it. HELP.

Dear 'Weight worrier' – I know how you feel. But we all have to eat in order to survive, and that is far, far more important than worrying about being overweight. Food should be fun, after all, and if you take exercise as well as eating a fairly healthy, normal diet – with five pieces of fruit or vegetable a day and not bingeing on choccies, etc. – you should be fine.

Dear Dr Ann – **I want to exercise regularly but it is just so boring.** How do I make it more fun?

Dear 'Fun-loving exerciser' – I agree with you that some exercise can be boring, but it doesn't have to be. There are so many different ways to exercise I can't believe that you will find ALL of them boring. But you didn't say what types of exercise you have already tried. Try listing them all in alphabetical order – aerobics, badminton, basketball, baseball, cricket, cycling...running, swimming, tennis, etc., and give them a fun rating from 1 to 5. I'm sure you'll find one you like. Some people find exercise is more fun if you do it with other people, while others prefer doing it on

their own. Most people who do some exercise feel better, are less depressed and generally have more fun.

It's supposed to be because some feel-good hormones called endorphins are released during exercise. Make sure you do 20 to 30 minutes of some sort of exercise most days and it'll even help you pass your exams!

Dear Dr Ann – **I'm a veggie and my friends think that I am anorexic because I don't eat very much** but I know that I eat loads really. What should I do, should I listen to them and eat more because I am fine about the food I eat and enjoy it.

Dear 'Veggie' – Just because you are a vegetarian does not mean you are anorexic. However, people who are anorexic tend to concentrate on eating vegetables rather than other foods like meat because they are lower in calories. But perhaps you should ask why your friends are worried? If you are really sure that you are eating loads and are fine about food and that your diet is a balance of vegetables, cheese, eggs, fruit, nuts, etc., then don't take any notice of what your friends are saying or thinking.

● EATING DISORDERS

The two common eating problems that young people suffer from are anorexia and bulimia, and excessive concern about body shape and weight are common to both. Both occur more in girls than boys – about 4 in 100 girls will have some type of eating disorder. Anorexics are very controlled about what they eat and get very thin and underweight. Bulimics are usually of normal weight and go in for binge-eating and dieting.

Dear Dr Ann – **I think I'm too fat because I eat too many sweets,** but can't stop it. I've tried eating the right sorts of food, and I did lose a bit of weight, but not enough. Then I did exercise but I just ached all over, so last week I got so fed up I went and bought some laxatives but they just made me sit on the loo for hours. I even tried making myself sick but it wouldn't come up. Please tell me how to lose weight as I look at my body and cry.

Dear 'Person taking laxatives' – It sounds like you're getting into a real state. First thing – throw those laxatives away, they won't help. Laxatives, starving yourself and making yourself sick is a really dangerous way to go – it can make you anorexic. The best way to lose weight is to love your body into fitness, not starving it to death. Take a look at what you are eating and when. Start keeping a food diary for a few days and make sure you eat three regular meals a day with a snack of fruit between, to stop you getting very hungry and reaching for the sweet tin.

Dear Dr Ann – **I think I'm becoming bulimic.** I make myself sick 3 times a day. i love the feeling of knowing that whatever i eat i can flush it down the toilet. Is that okay?

Dear 'Person with bulimia' – No, it's not OK, and yes, you do sound as if you are bulimic. Although your vomiting may seem like the main problem, actually the main problem is your dieting. When you diet, you put strict rules on yourself. When you can't stick to those rules because they are too strict and you are always feeling hungry, you have to break them – by eating a biscuit, perhaps, or a piece of chocolate. Then you overdo it and have a big binge – and then you vomit to try and get rid of all the calories you took in on your binge. But however much you vomit, you can only get rid of 50% of the calories that you have taken in, so people who have bulimia tend not to lose weight. So ease up on the diet, and try to eat regular meals so you don't get so hungry – include a snack between meals. Keep a detailed diary of all you eat and drink. Weigh yourself only once a week, as normal weight varies from day to day. Find alternatives to bingeing, like going for a walk, ringing a friend or some other distraction. Make a list of foods that that you think you should never eat, and try eating a little of them. This way you'll come to think about food more normally. Meanwhile, there is a very good book you might try to read called Overcoming Binge Eating, by Chris Fairbairn. It explains all about binge-eating – why you do it and how to stop.

Dear Dr Ann – **can you die of anorexia?**

Dear 'Concerned about dying from anorexia' – The
simple answer is yes, people do die from anorexia, by
literally starving themselves to death. One in five people with
anorexia severe enough for them to need to be admitted to
hospital will die from it. If you are worried that you have got
anorexia, stop pretending it's not a problem and please tell
your mum, dad, school nurse or another adult you trust. You
will need to go and get some help quickly.

Eating right

*You don't have to be very particular and know a lot about food to have a decent
diet that will keep you healthy. Best is to try to eat five portions of fruit and
vegetables a day, as well as all the other food you eat. A portion is an apple, a
pear, an orange, two tomatoes, or a handful of peas, beans or any other vegetable.
Try to eat meat that isn't too fatty. Chicken, turkey and fish are good unless they
are coated in lots of batter and breadcrumbs. Anything grilled is better than fried
food, as it tends to be less fatty. Pasta is good unless it is smothered in lots of fatty
cheddar cheese.*

IT AIN'T COMPLICATED, SO GIVE IT A GO.

For more information check out the www.doctorann.org website.

14 CLUED UP, NOT B'OOZED UP

The facts about alcohol...

Alcohol in reasonably small amounts can be terrific stuff and can:
- make parties go with a bang
- make you feel at ease when talking to people
- make you generally feel good
- help prevent heart disease when you are older (red wine that is!)

But with even moderate amounts of alcohol you can:
- be dangerous driving a car
- become increasingly violent
- have difficulties getting an erection

With binge-drinking you can:
- end up in hospital with alcohol poisoning
- become unconscious, inhale your vomit and die

With long-term drinking you can:
- affect babies inside the womb and damage their brains
- permanently destroy your liver cells
- permanently damage your health in other ways

A unit of alcohol is contained in half a pint of beer or in a 'short' of a spirit like gin, vodka or whisky. Girls can occasionally handle between 2 and 3 units a day, lads 4 or so, but certainly NOT every night. Any more and you start to get health problems.

Dear Dr Ann – **How much alcohol is a sensible amount to have at a party** to relax and feel good without puking it all up again the next morning. Is there a 'danger' limit or any rules to drink by? From Smirnoff ice fan.

> *Dear 'Smirnoff ice fan'* – It's nice to be able to enjoy parties in a relaxed way without actually needing alcohol. OK, OK, so many of us do like a bit of help! The problem is that alcohol doesn't only make you feel relaxed but it also lowers what are sensible inhibitions – like saying no to illegal drugs and no to unwanted sexual advances. You are also more likely to get into a fight or have an accident. So how much is it sensible to drink at a party? Probably not more than three units in an evening – a unit being HALF a pint of beer or one glass of wine or a small measure of Smirnoff. It's also a good idea to drink lots and lots of non-alcoholic drinks at the same time.

Dear Dr Ann – I have been having a slight problem recently **each time i go out with friends i drink too much and become out of control.** My boyfriend is great and takes care of me when this happens. When it does happen i do things i regret and i want this to stop but i will feel unhappy without alcohol and will not enjoy myself as much. Please help me.

> *Dear 'Out of control with alcohol'* – It sounds as though you are using alcohol as a prop when you feel nervous – which many of us do. But instead of being a prop, it is actually giving you more problems. Some practical tips: eat before you go out, and drink lots of non-alcoholic drinks before you go out. This way you won't just drink alcohol because you are thirsty, and the food will help dilute the alcohol you do take in. Pace yourself when you are out drinking, and make sure that for

every alcoholic drink you have, you also have a non-alcoholic one. Get the friends you go out with to help you by asking them to buy you non-alcoholic drinks. Alert your friends to how anxious you feel when you are out with them – because discussing it with them will make you feel less anxious.

Strength of alcoholic drinks

Ordinary beer is about 3.5% alcohol, strong lager and alcopops about 4–5%, and cider anything from 3–8%. Tennent's Super Strong lager is a whopping 9% – almost as strong as wine. Even stronger are sherry and port (17–20% alcohol), while spirits like whisky, gin or vodka are about 40%. Luckily, you almost never get pure alcohol, except in white spirit for cleaning paintbrushes, and most people sensibly stay away from drinking it – because it kills you!

Dear Dr Ann – **i know this might sound dumb** but about 3 weeks ago i went to this huge party and **drank WAY too much!!** I was sick afterwards which was horrible but i love the feeling of being a bit drunk. There's another party coming up but i don't want to drink so much that i'm sick again, how much is sensible and what's the suggested limit? From girl age14.

Dear 'Sick after drinking' – You're right that a little alcohol can make you feel good. Three units of alcoholic drink in an evening is enough and shouldn't make you sick or take silly risks. Make sure you have some food before you go to the party – don't drink on an empty stomach. Other tips are to sip rather than gulp the alcoholic drinks and to alternate them with other non-alcoholic drinks like water and fruit juices. Then you'll enjoy the party rather than ending up in the loo vomiting.

Dear Dr Ann – **a few nights ago i drunk about 1 litre** of vodka then went on to have **12 shots of dark rum** (YUK!). I seem to do this every other week. My dad said that i am lucky to be alive. Is this true and can you die from only drinking this much alcohol. From a drunkun git.

Listen, 'Drunkun Git' – If you go on this way, one of these days you WILL kill yourself with drink – probably more by accident than design. Technically, drinking between 300 and 500 cc (0.3–0.5 litre) of absolute alcohol in less than an hour will kill you. Spirits like gin, whisky and vodka are up to 55% pure alcohol – so you can work out for yourself how close you got. People die from alcohol because (a) alcohol suppresses the bit of your brain that keeps you breathing; or (b) you go into a coma, vomit and then choke on your vomit; or (c) your blood pressure goes very low, so all your vital organs don't get enough blood/oxygen. We all enjoy a little alcohol, and some of it is even good for you – but you sound as if you are behaving like a lunatic!

Dear Dr Ann – **does your liver ever recover from alcohol damage?**

Dear 'Worried about alcohol and liver damage' – The good news for your liver is that if you stop drinking, your liver cells do recover – as long as you haven't damaged them too much in the first place with large amounts of alcohol over a long period of time. Occasionally drinking 2-3 units in an evening is probably OK if you are under the age of 18.

● SOBERING UP – THIS WEEK OR NEXT?

Dear Dr Ann – **When they say that it takes 6 hours to sober up after drinking 6 units** does that mean it takes 6 hours to feel totally normal again or six hour to get back your senses?

Dear 'Alcohol wonderer' – Two things on this: first, the six hours means that you should NOT be driving within this time, because you may well still be over the limit; and secondly, you will probably still feel distinctly unwell up to this time and may well have a hangover lasting even longer! One thing that can help is to drink lots

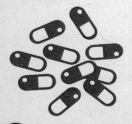

and lots of water, and paracetamol may help the headache (make sure you read the instructions to find the right dose). Don't start drinking alcohol again to make yourself feel better – even if you feel tempted. It will make you feel worse in the long run!

Dear Dr Ann – **What gets rid of alcohol fast?** I went round to a friend's house last night and we sort of got pissed on his dad's tennents extra. And now my head hurts and my mouth tastes of sludge. I'm drinking black coffee but I still feel awful – from spaced out girl.

Dear 'Spaced-out girl' – I'm afraid there aren't any short cuts, but drinking water will help the headache. It's a myth that black coffee, showers, a fry-up or more drink help – there's no way to sober up quickly. Sounds like you've got a bit of a hangover? Tennent's Extra is pretty strong stuff. You're probably feeling awful because your liver's exhausted from processing all that alcohol, and your head's all dried out.

If you think you have a drinking problem, then DRINKLINE's young people's service is on 0800 917 8282.

15 BLOWING YOUR MIND?

What's legal, what's illegal, and where to find out more

Drugs are substances that have an effect on your mind and body and the way they work. There are lots of different types, both legal and illegal. Some, like caffeine (in tea and coffee) and alcohol, we hardly think of as drugs at all. Then there are legal drugs, like paracetamol, that you can buy 'over the counter' at your chemist's. You can also get 'prescribed' drugs, like penicillin, from the chemist, but you have to have a prescription from your doctor. Finally there is a whole range of illegal drugs, including amphetamines, ecstasy, cocaine and heroin. Cannabis is also an illegal drug, but the law has recently changed so that you are less likely to be arrested for having small amounts for personal use. However, remember even cannabis can have harmful effects.

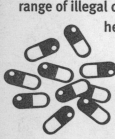

Around three quarters of young people in the UK will be offered drugs before they are 16, and around half will experiment with them. Luckily almost all this experimentation will be with cannabis. Of those experimenting with illegal drugs, around 1 in 20 will go on to get into serious long-term problems with them.

DRUGS: SOFT, NOT SO SOFT, AND THEIR EFFECT

Dear Dr Ann – **I need some information on caffeine** but it isn't anywhere. is it a drug? can you help? 17 year old male.

Dear 'Wanting to know about caffeine' – Yes, caffeine is a drug in that it can alter your perceptions of the outside world, but it is a legal one, of course. It is found in tea, coffee, Coca-Cola and many other drinks, as well as in some pills. It acts on your brain and stimulates it. Some people are more sensitive than others to caffeine and find that if they take too much they feel all hyped-up. A lot of caffeine can also make your heart beat fast, and some people find that if they have drinks containing caffeine, they get very jumpy and nervous.

Dear Dr Ann – **i've been hanging around with some pretty rough people** for quite some time & they drop pills, smoke weed & drink heavily & i've started doin all that. the lad that i'm seeing is worried 'bout me & i don't know whether to stop for him. what should i do because i dont wanna lose him.

Dear 'Hanging around with a rough lot' – It sounds as if your lad has more sense than the people you have been hanging around with. It is your life – you are the only one who can decide and I think you know what you should do. And then you won't lose him.

Hi *dr ann* – **my mate is doing drugs.** what can i do to stop him?

Dear 'Mate of a mate doing drugs' – Around half of all teenagers will experiment with illegal drugs and half will stay well away from them. Most of this 'experimenting' will be smoking a bit of cannabis. What you really need to worry about is whether your mate is actually hooked on drugs. Best thing is to talk to him about it, and try and find out why he is doing them. You may not be able to get him to stop, but it will certainly help him to have someone he can talk to about it.

'Scuse me Dr Ann – **but how do drugs affect babies?**

Dear 'Person interested in drugs and babies' – I assume you mean unborn babies developing inside their mothers? There is a wide range of drugs, both legal and illegal, that can affect the unborn baby. In general, it is best not to use any legal or illegal drugs during early pregnancy, unless you have to for medical reasons. Illegal drugs almost all affect people's brains – and the brains of developing babies inside the uterus (womb) are particularly sensitive.

● DOPE, POT, WEED, GRASS...

Cannabis comes from the hemp plant. It contains something called THC (tetrahydrocannabinols), which is the chemical that has the effect. It has more names than most people have had hot dinners, including dope, pot, weed, grass, green, hash, marijuana, blow, draw, rocky, black, leb, gear and puff. Normally it either looks like dried-up grass or comes in a hard block. It is usually smoked but can also be eaten. It has recently been downgraded as an illegal drug, and most people found using it but not 'dealing' would not now be cautioned or arrested. If you are dealing, then expect trouble and a long prison sentence.

Dear Dr Ann – **please, please can you help? – it's my mate. i think he's on dope.** He's got in with a bad crowd and when I saw him on Saturday and yesterday he was just dozy, like he couldn't really care I was there. Also I'm worried he's going to try heroin and cocaine and all that as well.

Dear 'Worried about dopey mate' – Cannabis can make you feel better for a bit, but it only makes you feel better because you stop noticing the bad stuff – it doesn't make the bad stuff go away. And you can see the bad effects on your mate – dozy, can't remember much. Most people who try cannabis just do it to experiment and don't go on to try harder stuff, but some do. But it sounds as though your friend might need help. It's a hard choice – if you grass him up (excuse the pun), he might get thrown out of school. If you don't, he might just carry on being whacked out all the time. Is there some adult you trust who you can discuss his problem with, perhaps without saying who he is?

Dear Dr Ann – **all me mates smoke the weed from time to time, and I do it with them sometimes, but I'm not sure about it.** Could you tell me more about the stuff please? Boy 15.

Dear 'Weeder' – Cannabis has been smoked for many years by millions of people. But because it is illegal in most countries, there hasn't been all that much decent research done on its effects – although there is a huge amount of hearsay and myth. There is still a great deal of debate about how 'dangerous' a drug cannabis is. If you smoke cannabis, it starts having an effect after a few minutes and the effect can last up to three hours; but if you have a bad time with it, it can take much longer to wear off. It can have very different effects on different people:

- you may feel great – happy, relaxed, talkative and giggly
- you may feel you are much more aware of what's going on around you
- you may feel anxious, confused, withdrawn, depressed, and that everyone is getting at you
- you may feel a combination of these things.

If you use a lot:
- you begin to...oh, yeah...sort of...um...forget things
- you lose your...what's it called? That thing...um, er...concentration
- this can give you trouble with your schoolwork and your social life.

In fact, you can become a real 'druggie', and in certain cases cannabis use is linked with serious mental health problems. If you tend to get a bit depressed or anxious anyhow, then cannabis can make it worse.

Dear Dr Ann – **I have been smoking marijuana** for a week now and feel constantly stoned, is there something terribly wrong with me?

Dear 'Marijuana smoker' – What is wrong with you is the fact that you could possibly imagine that if you smoke marijuana for a week, you won't feel stoned for a week! Stop smoking the marijuana and you won't feel stoned. The marijuana seems to be making you lose your common sense!

● THE AGONY AND THE...

The medical name for E, or ecstasy, is MDMA (the first initials of a hugely long chemical name), and it comes in tablets with pictures stamped on it. MDMA tells your brain to flood itself with massive amounts of serotonin, the natural chemical that keeps you happy. Then your tanks are empty and you feel grotty for days while your brain makes some more. Scientists think that large amounts of ecstasy may damage your brain's serotonin system permanently.

Dear Dr Ann – **What is the effect of ecstasy?**

Dear 'Effects of ecstasy wonderer' – Well, there are a whole lot of things one could say about it – and most of these you can find by clicking on 'ecstasy' on my www.doctorann.org website. But here are some facts anyhow. It comes as a white tablet which normally contains very little of the active stuff. The drug itself releases chemical messengers in the brain called serotonin. This stuff normally helps control your mood – how hungry, aggressive, sexy, etc. you feel. The REAL problem is that no one knows what long-term damage the drug does to your brain, but the more research that is done, the more likely it seems that it is doing harm. One very rare and very serious affect is that it can cause you either to lose an enormous amount of sweat dancing away to music while the ecstasy is driving you, or to take in too much water to compensate for this. Both of these things have occasionally caused ecstasy users to die.

Dear Dr Ann – Last night we went clubbing with my mate. **She said she'd got some E off her brother and it was giving her the best night of her life.** Well we were dancing and then she just lost it, came back to us and fell over. They had to call the ambulance. What went wrong? From Oasis fan.

Dear 'Oasis fan with friend on E' – I hope that your friend is OK now. It sounds like she collapsed from overheating – heatstroke. E stops you feeling tired, so you dance and dance in an overcrowded and overheated club and then suddenly your body can't take any more. It's very scary. If you know someone's on E, make sure they chill out every hour or so somewhere cool, and that they drink water regularly – up to a pint an hour. If they collapse, take them somewhere cool (not freezing), loosen their clothes and splash water on them. Stick with them till help arrives, as they may be having nightmares.

Amphetamines bought on the street are usually less than 10% amphetamine – the rest is stuff like caffeine, baking soda and sugar, as well as de-worming powder and other yucky stuff. Amphetamine ('speed') normally comes as a white powder, in tablets or in capsules, and you can sniff it, swallow it, smoke it or inject it. Injecting it, or anything else, is mad.

Dear Dr Ann – **is Dexy's bad 4 U?** My brother does it and says it's great and he's always jumping around like shit and he can't stop jittering and shivering and thinking of something else and I want 2 know if he's right.

Dear 'Brother on Dexy's' – No, Dexy's aren't good for you – they send your poor heart manic and you can't calm down. Dexy's are amphetamines, and they all work the same way – make you hyper, talking 19 to the dozen, whizzing round the dance floor. He probably thinks he's Roadrunner. The trouble with speed – and with most drugs – is that you can't actually get real with someone on them. They just grin and don't listen. The down from speed is bad. You feel like you're drowning in black treacle – heavy, exhausted, depressed. Some people who use it a lot have also got really moody and paranoid.

All illegal drugs are bad for you but some are worse than others. The really, really nasty illegal drugs include cocaine, crack and heroin. These are highly addictive, and whatever other people tell you, start on these and you are likely to end up unhappy, losing friends, short of money, stealing, and getting in with criminals – basically a really sad person.

You can get more information about illegal drugs by going to www.doctorann.org or emailing info@release.org.uk. Or you can phone Release at 0207 729 9904.

16 YOUR FUTURE UP IN SMOKE?

Why people smoke and the effects it has

People tend to try smoking because (a) friends do it, (b) they think it makes them look 'hard' or 'cool', (c) they enjoy experimenting with different things, (d) they feel it makes them more self-confident, (e) they think it helps them concentrate, and (f) they think it helps keep them thin. In fact, the effects of smoking are: every cigarette you smoke knocks five minutes off your life; it makes you stink; it makes it more difficult for boys to get erections; it damages your baby if you are pregnant; it affects your blood vessels; it makes it more likely that you will get high blood pressure; it gives you lung cancer; it wastes your money.

● GETTING STARTED, GETTING ADDICTED

Dear Dr Ann – **If you try a fag do you get addicted straightaway?** And how many fags does it take to get addicted?

Dear 'Fags and addiction' – The latest research suggests that smoking between two and five cigarettes is enough to start getting you hooked. Everyone thinks that, when they first try smoking, they won't have a problem stopping again, but tobacco appears to be at least as addictive as the illegal drug heroin. Even so, most people who really, really want to stop smoking can, and things like nicotine patches or gum definitely help. Addiction is funny because it isn't 'all or nothing' – how addicted someone gets depends on the individual and his or her personality. The reason why you want to smoke also plays a part. Remember, it's never too late to give up, but no one is pretending that it may not be hard to do.

Dear Dr Ann – **My friend is slightly plump and has started smoking cigarettes.** She'll go through a pack of 20 every night when she is with her friends except when she is with me. I think she is doing it because she wants to look hard and get popular, or to try and get thin, which isn't working very well.

Dear 'Friend of plump smoker' – Lots of people start smoking because they think it will make them look hard, and lots of girls start because they think it will help them get thin. Smoking doesn't make you thin – it just costs a lot of money, makes your breath smell bad, and means that you are addicted to something that is very, very hard to give up. When you do give up, you tend to put on weight for a bit because you tend to eat more trying to get over the tobacco addiction. With all the health problems that we know smoking causes, it makes people look stupid rather than hard. I've got some tips that might help your friend – you'll find them at the end of the chapter.

Half of all smokers are eventually killed by the tobacco they smoke. Those who die from smoking lose on average 16 years of their life. But if you smoke and you manage to stop by the age of 25, then you don't run any increased risk of dying early. And if you stop before the age of 30, you avoid over 90% of the risk of tobacco-induced lung cancer. Of course smoking kills even more people as a result of diseases other than lung cancer, but these risks are largely avoided by stopping in time.

• AND IT ISN'T JUST SMOKERS WHO SUFFER

Dear Dr Ann – **My brothers and step dad all smoke and I breathe in smoke** and now I have got a really bad cough. What shall I do?

Dear 'Passive smoker' – You have every right to feel furious with your brothers and step-dad. Apart from anything else, it is horrid having to smell all the cigarette smoke in your hair, clothes, furniture and everything. They are being mean and thoughtless, and they could be damaging your health if you are coughing, though coughs can be caused by lots of different things. Is there someone else in the house who doesn't smoke? Gang up on your brothers and step-dad and get them to smoke outside or in just one room in the house.

● IF YOU WANT TO STOP...

Dear Dr Ann – **How do I stop smoking?** I know it's bad for me but I kinda like it as well. Yeah, and look, I don't need a lecture, I want some help. Even though I know it's bad for me, I actually feel better when I smoke. So how do I quit and still feel OK? From marlboro girl.

> *Dr A: Fine* – **then the way to stop is by wanting to stop more than you want to smoke. So let's figure out why you want to smoke – apart from the physical addiction in nicotine. How did you become marlboro girl in the first place?**

MG: Well about 4 years ago when I was 12. I was hanging round with these older girls called Cheri and Joanna. They lit up and said, 'don't you want one?' So I sucked on a cig and coughed and cried and spluttered and said 'ooh, that was great'. All that summer we kept hanging out together, and when they smoked I did too. Then when we went back to school I started going out with this really nice guy called Scott. He didn't like the taste so I stopped and it wasn't too bad – I'd rather pucker up for him than a fag.

> *Dr A:* **Sounds great. What went wrong?**

MG: We split up that Christmas. He was my first serious boy and it really sent me down. I was sitting in my room crying and I thought, 'I need a cigarette to cope with this'. So now I've been smoking about 10 a day.

> *Dr A:* **What about your family? Do they mind?**

MG: Well, they know I smoke a few, but not nearly as many as I really do. I don't smoke in the house. I go outside, in the park, with my friends, in the clubs.

> *Dr A:* **So why do you want to give up?**

MG: Why do you think? You're the doc.

> *Dr A:* **Well, lots of reasons. For your health, to save money, to smell nicer...**

MG: I have a cough to kill me, I'm short of breath every time I run for the bus. I can't walk round town all day with my friends – I have to sit down and then I have another fag.

Dr A: And why do you like smoking?

MG: Well...I feel quite calm with a cigarette around. It helps me take a step back and look at the world and see what's going on.

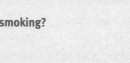

Dr A: So you think you look good smoking?

MG: Yeah, I suppose so.

Dr A: Well, if feeling relaxed and cool is what keeps you smoking, then you need to figure out how to have your moments of feeling relaxed and cool and not smoke. The times when you normally smoke are the difficult ones to get through. But if you know when they are, you can work out ways through them. So – any ideas on how to chill out without lighting up?

MG: No, not really. I suppose I could try deep breathing or something.

Dr A: That's a very good idea. Slow, deep breathing calms you down and helps you step out of life for a moment. Anything else?

MG: Mmm. Not really.

Dr A: I'd suggest you get something ready to do as well: call a friend on your mobile, buy a mag, chew gum, write a letter to someone you miss, do some exercise...whatever. Just don't get bored and start thinking about smoking.

MG: I haven't got a mobile.

Dr A: Ah, but if you quit smoking for a week, you'll save £14. Three weeks is £42, which should mean you'll be able to buy a phone and tell everyone else on the bus about your love life pretty soon.

MG: OK. Are those nicotine patch things any good?

Dr A: Yes, they are. Not everyone needs them but some people like them. Best of all, tell people you're quitting. Then they can encourage you along.

MG: Yeah. I hadn't thought of that. My mum will be pleased.

Dr A: No more sneaking out in the rain for a fag... no more making sure you've always got a few on you... no more sitting in class dying for one... you'll be pleased too.

MG: Hey – how do you know all this?

Dr A: Having lots of smokers in my surgery, that's how! I'll email you in a week and see how you're doing.

Tips for quitting

- 👁 You have to want to.
- 👁 Pick a day and quit. Then keep quitting the next day. Then the next. One day at a time.
- 👁 Realize that you'll feel pissed off, trembly and anxious for a while. That's the nicotine, pestering you like your annoying kid sister. Ignore it. Like your kid sister, it'll go away after a while.
- 👁 Think of times when you normally smoke – parties, just before bed, with your friends. Work out how to get through them without smoking. Chew some gum, play with a Gameboy, learn to play the harmonica – anything that keeps your hands busy and your mind awake. Nicotine patches, gum and stuff all help and cost less than the fags.
- 👁 Find a friend who also wants to give up, and quit together.
- 👁 Avoid friends who push cigarettes on you. Usually they want you to keep smoking so they don't feel so bad about smoking themselves.
- 👁 Don't worry about gaining weight – even if you do, you'll lose it again as you get fitter.
- 👁 Feel proud that you're not paying money to big companies that grow their tobacco by cutting down forests, creating deserts, etc.
- 👁 If you fail, don't worry. Think why you failed. Work out how you can win next time. Then quit again.
- 👁 Treat yourself to something really expensive – present, meal, whatever takes your fancy – with all the money you've saved. You deserve it!

ARE THE TOUGH GUYS REALLY SO TOUGH?

Things you should know about bullies and bullying

Bullying happens when someone or a group of people do nasty things to you or keep on teasing or harassing you in a way that you don't like. About half of all boys and girls are bullied at school at some time. The really crazy thing is that people who have been bullied themselves are more likely to go on to bullying others. Bullies tend not to like school, so maybe they feel generally fed up with life and want to take it out on other people. Bullies at school are four times more likely to become criminals than non-bullies.

It doesn't seem to matter what colour you are or what culture or race you come from, the rate of bullying is roughly the same. Not surprisingly, being bullied at school can make you not want to go to school, so it is one of the reasons for boys and girls truanting.

Hi Dr Ann – **Why do people bully?**

Dear 'Concerned about bullying' – A bully is a person who uses their strength or power in order to frighten or intimidate people. Unfortunately, we probably all behave in ways that those around us think of as bullying at some time or other. People who persistently bully, however, are often those who have been bullied themselves, or lack self-confidence – it makes them feel good to exert power over others.

Dear Dr Ann – **Nobody likes me even though I am always nice to them.** I am constantly being rejected from various social activities and it is really getting me down. It seems like all the nasty people get all the friends. Male age 15.

Dear 'Feeling rejected' – I'm not surprised that you're feeling rejected if it's really true that nobody likes you. But I am sure that it just feels like that at the moment. Give up trying to be friends with the 'nasty people' who are excluding you from things – it sounds like they are unkind and possibly behaving like bullies. I am sure you will find there are other people you can do things with, once you give up trying to get in with a crowd who for whatever reason don't want you. Try joining in with people who have some of the same interests as you. And remember, even if other people seem part of the in-crowd, they may not feel it inside – we all feel outsiders and rejected at some time in our lives, especially when we are depressed or aren't feeling good about ourselves in other ways. But do talk your parents or someone else you can trust about how you feel. Sharing the hurt often helps.

Dear Dr Ann – **I hate being bullied.** It makes me feel lonely. Something needs to be done about it.

Dear 'Bullied and lonely' – Yes, of course, everyone hates being bullied, but the question here is what can you do about it. Have you tried talking to someone about it – at school, at home, with friends or with other members of your family? Don't give in, and don't feel that you are alone with this, because unfortunately we almost all get bullied at one time or another. If you can talk to someone about, it will make you feel much less alone with your problem.

Dear Dr Ann – **i have been getting bullied in school and i cant sleep at night,** i have tried telling the teachers but they wont listen, so i told my parents, they came up to the school to sort things out but they still havnt done anything about it, what can i do.

Dear 'Bullied and sleepless' – So sorry to hear about your problems, it must be really horrid. Unfortunately, lots of people are bullied at school. First, don't give up – keep on telling people about it, especially your teachers and parents. You are not making an unnecessary fuss, especially as all schools are meant to have an anti-bullying policy. You should find out about this from your teachers. Second, try ringing Childline on 0800 1111 – it's free. Also, try sticking with a friend who is supportive of you, because bullies like to pick on people who appear vulnerable and on their own.

Dear Dr Ann – **i am being bullied.** these people are spreading rumours about me and my school wont do anything about it. i have told my year head and deputy head but they wont do anything to stop it. please help me cos i dont know wot to do!!

Dear 'Bullied and desperate' – Very, very sorry that no one is listening to you. Every school is meant to have a policy for dealing with bullying. However, given that you have tried that, have you tried getting your mum and dad involved and getting them to talk to the school about your problem? Otherwise try ringing Childline. They will listen to your problems, and being able to talk about them with someone often helps by itself. But they will probably be able to help you in other ways too.

Dear Dr Ann – **I have a bed wetting problem.** I confided in my friend about it a while ago. He is now hanging around with some other boys who he has told. They have told more people and i am worried that it will get out of control. Linkin Park Fan.

Dear 'Linkin Park fan' – I am so sorry you have been betrayed by a friend. This is another form of bullying really. People usually tell about this kind of thing when, for some reason or other, they feeling inadequate about themselves. They like to be nasty about other people's problems to make themselves feel good. Ignore him/them and don't tell him any more secrets. It's more than likely that some of the boys he has told have a bedwetting problem themselves, as it is not that uncommon even in teenagers. Bedwetting does usually get better by your late teens. It often runs in families and is more common in boys. There are things to try that might help.

Keep a diary and get your mum to give you a reward for every dry night. If this doesn't help, see your doc, who can arrange for you to have a special alarm you put in your bed under the sheet. It wakes you as you start to wet, so you can get up and piss in the toilet rather than in your bed. There are also some tablets or sprays you squirt up your nose which might help.

Dear Dr Ann – **I am an Asian living in a predominantly white area. I get beaten up and spat at** by people younger than me. I can't speak to anyone because they wouldn't understand. I feel really down and cry a lot because of it. Who can I tell and what can I do?

Dear 'Person being beaten up and spat at' – This is totally out of order and appears to be racist. You may not think that other people will understand, but they will – it's really just another form of bullying. Unfortunately, it seems to make rather inadequate people feel good to gang up together and bully others who are in some way different from them. Find someone to travel with you who will support you. It doesn't matter whether they are Asian, white or anything else – as long as they are against racism and bullying and are on your side. Remember, there are lots of people who feel very strongly anti-racist and anti-bullying – whatever their colour or race – and they will give you support.

What to do if you are being bullied or harassed:

- 👁 tell someone about it – mum, dad, friend, teacher, anyone/everyone that you trust – then work out with them the best way of dealing with the problem
- 👁 if you possibly can, try not to give in to threats – in most cases bullies will not carry out their threats, but when they know that you will give in to them, they will keep on bullying
- 👁 try not to show the bullies that you are afraid or that they are getting to you, because that is how they get their kicks
- 👁 try to stay out of the bullies' way, and if you can't, stick with your friends, as bullies only like to bully people who are alone
- 👁 write down somewhere the dates and times when you are bullied and what happened and show it to someone you trust – a record of what has been going on is very powerful in making people believe you
- 👁 be careful not to take out your feelings of being bullied by bullying other people who are worse off than you
- 👁 try ringing Childline on 0800 1111 or check out the Pupiline website on www.pupiline.net.

Dear Doc A – **At school and on the bus I get made fun of because my skin is very pale.** People call me 'Casper', 'Zombie' and 'Ghost boy'. This is making me feel very depressed. Help!!!

Dear 'Person with pale skin' – I am tempted to say 'just ignore them', but I know this won't help and is almost impossible. But don't let them see that you are upset by them or they will just pick on you more. This is clearly bullying and you need to tell someone (parents or school) about it. Find out what kind of anti-bullying policy you have at your school. The best of these policies get the students to decide how the bullies should be dealt with.

18 RU GAY, HOMOSEXUAL, LESBIAN?

Every combination happens...

There are young people who are sexually attracted to someone of their own sex and who think that they may be homosexual. Some boys are attracted to other boys and to girls, and some girls are attracted to other girls as well as boys – this is known as being 'bisexual'. Some men want to spend time dressed as women and some women want to spend time dressed as men – which is called 'cross-dressing'. Then there are people who want to actually change their sex – a boy wanting to be a girl or a girl wanting to be a boy.

In most cases it is not clear whether these attractions, needs or desires are driven by hormones, genes, upbringing or other things. Most probably there is a combination of different factors involved in each individual person – and the situation may be temporary or permanent. There are no absolute rights or wrongs about any of this.

Dear Doctor Ann – **how do you know if you are gay?** Boy aged 14.

Dear 'Wondering about being gay' – Many young
people wonder about this, both boys and girls.
Teenagers quite often go through a period when they
find their own sex attractive as well as the opposite sex,
but that doesn't make you gay. If you do find as you get
older that you are more and more strongly attracted to
someone of the same sex as you, it may mean you're
gay but you will just have to wait and see. Only about
one in 25 men and one in 50 women report having some
kind of homosexual experience between the ages of 16
and 19.

Dear Doctor Ann – **what is a lesbian?** Asked by: worried girl 13.

Dear 'Worried lesbian wonderer' – A lesbian is a girl or
woman who is sexually attracted to another girl or woman.
Women can be great friends with other women without being
lesbian. It is only when strong sexual feelings are involved, as
well as emotions like friendship and love, that it is called
lesbianism. According to the research, less than six in every 100
women, in a lifetime, have any kind of sexual feelings for another
woman.

Dear Doctor Ann – **Am i a lesbian?** I am 12 years old and i think i might be a lesbian. I
like the look of women's bodies and i don't know what is wrong with me! Help!!!

Dear 'Person who likes the look of women's bodies' –
Liking the look of women's bodies doesn't necessarily make
you a lesbian. But you may need to wait till you are a bit older
to find out whether you are more attracted to women or to
men. Lots of girls at around the time of puberty develop
'crushes' on other women, but few of them decide that they
are lesbian when they become adults.

Dear Doctor Ann – **I think I'm gay.** I'm still a virgin and there is no one that I can turn to for help. There are no organizations in my local area for Gay people seeking advice and I wish I could meet someone in the same position as me. I'm feeling really lonely and depressed, what should I do? Boy 15.

Dear 'Wonderer about being gay' – Lots of young people think about this quite a bit, and it can make you feel quite isolated if you can't talk about it. Why not check out the facts on my www.doctorann.org website? If you want to talk about it further, try ringing the Lesbian and Gay Switchboard on 0207 837 7324. You won't have to give your name, and they have lots of information about local groups.

Dear Dr Ann – **how do you fix gayness?** Boy age 14.

Dear 'Gayness fixer' – If you mean by fixing gayness 'stopping yourself being sexually attracted to someone of the same sex', then I don't think it quite works like that. As they go through puberty, many boys and girls feel attracted to people of the same sex, but it doesn't necessarily mean that they are gay – though in a small number of cases it may. If you do find you are gay, you will gradually become aware of who you do feel sexually attracted to.

Dear Dr Ann – **I want to be a girl**, but i am too afraid to go to my family doctor about this so i decided to ask you: at what age could i start to take hormones? Age: 15 Sex: male.

Dear 'Boy wanting to be a girl' – It is not that uncommon to feel unsure or uncomfortable with your sexuality and have doubts about what you want to be. The important thing is not to do anything in a hurry. I'm afraid no one will give you hormones while you are so young, as the hormones you need to take are strong chemicals and can do harm. There's no definite age at which to get them, but you will need to discuss your feelings with an expert and think very seriously about it all for some years before taking such a step. There are experts to help you, and you should not feel alone. If you are afraid to see your own family doctor, you can change to another doctor, who will be able to arrange further help.

19 HAVE U BEEN SEXUALLY ABUSED?

How people who sexually abuse children or young people work

Unfortunately, it is almost inevitable that most girls and many boys in their teens will experience some form of sexual exposure from an adult, whether it is a flasher or being rubbed up against in a bus or in the underground. These experiences are virtually the norm, and if it happens to you, tell your family about it but don't let it get to you too much.

Men who sexually abuse children (and it is mainly men who do it) are very, very clever at getting children to trust them. They look for children who are friendly, receptive and vulnerable, and try to gain their confidence by developing a 'special relationship' with them. By the time the sexual abuse actually takes place, the child may feel that he or she has given their consent. The abusing adult then threatens that, should the child tell anyone about what is going on, the child or the abuser will suffer terribly. Never listen to this – always, always tell someone.

SEXUAL ABUSE

Dear Dr Ann – hello, i hope you can help me. My parents divorced when i was 9 because my dad has mental health problems and was medically retired. Soon after they divorced my mum began to see this bloke who was our plumber (respected, well known person etc). **When i was 13 he sexually abused me** for a few months in my room. I kept it quiet for a year whilst gradually falling to pieces. My friend told one of my close teachers that there was something up but had no idea what. I ended up confessing all to my teacher, and was told that if I did not tell my mum that evening she would. I told my mum and she reacted very badly, but when I came home my older brother told me that my mum had 'dumped' her boyfriend. A few weeks later I went to the police and gave details (against my mums wishes) but decided not to prosecute – also when questioned he denied it and sobbed. This was in the January and just before the summer I realised that she was still seeing him on the quiet – he lives less than a mile away. In the August my brother and I confronted her with it – and we had evidence – such things as letters which he wrote to her admitting everything and their plan to run off together. Even though she denied it we thought that she would stop because of fear of losing us. However by summer this year (1 year on) we knew that she was clearly still seeing him and confronted her again. My brother is at uni but any time he is around he lives mostly at his girlfriends so I am left alone with my mum trying to be civil...which just gets harder every day. PLEASE, what if anything can I do?? I'm 16 now, in my final year at school, I dont have any relatives and get no support at all with anything. PLEASE HELP.

Dear 'Sixteen-year-old on a bad break, who was sexually abused' – It is great that you've been brave enough to tell us your story because we feel that other people may have had a similar experience but find it too difficult to write about it. Your story will help them feel less alone with their problems. What this guy your mother has taken up with did is VERY, VERY WRONG, and you must feel very let down by the adults in your life, especially the ones who are responsible for you. You have

had to grow up with the fear that your mother may go off with someone who has sexually abused you, and you may feel that she loves him more than she loves you. I am sure that this is not true, but your mother sounds like a lonely person herself. So why don't you discuss how you feel about it all with her a bit more? I suggest that you talk to your brother first about it and that you and he tackle your mother together. You could also try talking to your family doctor about it all and see if she/he could arrange some counselling for you. It won't change what has happened but may help you come to terms with it.

Dear Dr Ann – I am a 13 year old boy and don't know who to tell this to. My parents want me to pass my GCSEs so they are sending me to a man who is meant to be helping me with my maths. But **he is touching my willie and wants me to touch his** – and I don't want to.

Dear 'Person being sexually abused' – First, IT IS NOT YOUR FAULT. Next, DON'T DO ANYTHING YOU DON'T WANT TO DO. You could start by refusing to go and see this man. Tell someone about what is happening now. Best would be your parents, even if you feel a bit embarrassed – they would want to know. Keep telling people about it till someone does something about it, because it must stop. If you have already talked with your parents about sex using words like penis and vagina, you will be able to use these words more easily. Then, if something you don't like happens to you, you can talk to your parents about it without so much embarrassment.

● EMAIL EXCHANGE: A BOY'S STORY

Saw some stuff on TV about those children in Wales who were abused, and want to talk to someone about it. Can it be you, or should it be someone else. Will you email me.

Yes, Jake. What would you like to tell me about?

Well I don't know really, I mean, it may be that it's O.K. but I don't like it.

Jake, what don't you like?

I live with my mum and her boyfriend and he touches me like.

Can you tell me a bit more, Jake?

Well like when my mum is out he makes me touch his thing and he touches mine.

Jake, is he getting you to touch his penis and is he touching your penis?

Yes, and I don't think it's right.

No, it is not right. Thank you for telling me about it. Have you been able to tell anyone else about this?

No, mum's boyfriend says he'll kill me if I do, and I can't tell mum can I, cos he's her boyfriend and maybe he'll hurt her too.

Jake, I am so sorry this is happening to you. You need to tell another grown-up about these things. You need someone you can trust. Do you have a family friend or relative who you get on well with, or is there a teacher at school who you trust and can talk to?

My form teacher at school. She's OK.

OK, tell her about it if you can. She will have to tell someone else – perhaps someone who works for social services – and they will make it stop happening. Jake, thank you for telling me about it. If it doesn't work – if you find you can't tell your form teacher, or she doesn't do anything about it – then contact me again and I will tell you some more things to try. In the meantime you could ring CHILDLINE on 0800 1111.

● EMAIL EXCHANGE: A GIRL'S STORY

Dear Dr Ann – can I talk to you a moment, from Sally (it's not my real name though)

Hello Sally, what would you like to talk about?

It's about my friend, she wants to run away and go to Barbados.

I know the feeling – but why Barbados in particular?

So that she can lie on a beach and get a beautiful tan and swim and be clean.

Mmm. Does she want to be clean and beautiful because at home she feels ugly and dirty?

I think maybe.

Do you know anything that is making her feel that way?

She's got a new stepdad and she doesn't like him.

What's wrong with him? Is he a horrible person?

Well hes very big and laughs a lot and drives a Porshe.

That doesn't sound like a reason to hate someone – apart from the Porsche, obviously.

But he doesnt laugh at home and he hurts her mum and stuff.

Oh dear. That sounds nasty. Does he do things to your friend that she doesn't like as well?

Yes. He...

He does what, Sally?

He kisses her when he puts her to bed.

And is that the only thing that makes her feel ugly and dirty? Does he touch her in the wrong places too?

Yes.

Sally, can I ask you how old your friend is?

She's 13.

And has she told her mum about what he does, do you think?

No, he says its their own secret from mum.

OK – well, Sally, I am so sorry for her, because what her stepdad is doing is wrong, and it's not her fault. Really it isn't. Do you think she knows that – could you tell her that?

I'll try.

You've already been very brave to write to me about it, but in order to stop him, you also need to tell another adult about it. If you are close to your mum, you could tell her. If you can't tell your mum, tell some other grown-up – a close grown-up friend if you have one, an aunt or a teacher.

I dont think they'd believe me.

Well, the law says that a teacher has to listen and take you seriously if you tell him or her what you've told me. But if she wants, your friend could go with her mum to the doctor. She could say it's because she's really hurting badly. Then she could ask the doctor to get her mum to leave the room, so it's just her telling the doctor. The doctor will stop it from happening, but she/he may have to tell someone else – maybe her mum, if your friend agrees – in order to make it stop happening.

But I don't want to hurt my mum! Oops I meant to say 'her' mum, but you might as well know.

It's OK, Sally, I guessed who you were really talking about. But your mum doesn't want you to be feeling ugly and dirty, does she? So please, be brave and tell someone you trust. That way you can be free from what your stepdad has been doing.

● VIOLENCE AND RAPE

Dear Dr Ann – **I was raped on holiday 2 weeks ago**, i've told my boyfriend and he's helped me through it. I can't seem to stop thinking about it, i'm going back to school tomorrow and don't know how i'll concentrate.

Dear 'Worried because of being raped' – You do need to do something about it URGENTLY because, apart from your emotional upset, you are at real risk of either being pregnant or having got a sexually transmitted disease. The best thing would be to phone the Brook Advisory Service on 0800 0185 023 or the Rape Crisis Centre on 0207 278 3956 – NOW. You may want to think about telling the police about it too, in order to make sure that he doesn't rape anyone else.

Dear Dr Ann – **My mum and dad split up and ever since I've lived with dad. The thing is he's started to beat me up** and things. I don't know what to do, as he hits me with anything and everything. I need your help as he doesn't stop. I hate him. The thing that is really important is that he raped me and I can't get it off my mind and even when I try it's still there. My brother is 16 and he doesn't know about it. Should I tell him? I am aged 13.

Dear '13-year-old being beaten by her dad' – Certainly tell your brother and ask him to get help for you. Otherwise tell your mum, if you are still seeing her, or anyone else you trust. Finally you should try ringing Childline on 0800 1111 (it's free) and talk to them about it. Or try their website www.childline.org.uk. Take care.

Things to do if you are being sexually or physically abused:

- *if you can, avoid any further contact with the person who is abusing you*
- *if you can't avoid seeing them, tell the person who is doing it that you don't like it and to stop – and keep on saying it again and again and again*
- *tell another person about it, and keep on telling people about it till someone does something about it*
- *try ringing Childline on 0800 1111 and tell them about it*

Need to find out more?

Teenage Health Freak

The Diary of a Teenage Health Freak
(3rd edition, OUP 2002)
The book that got it all going. Read the latest version of Pete Payne's celebrated diary in all its gory detail, to find out pretty much all you need to know about your health, your body and how it works (or doesn't – whatever).

The Diary of the Other Health Freak
(3rd edition, OUP 2002)
The book that kept it all going. Pete's sister Susie sets out to outshine her big brother with a diary of her own, bringing the feminine touch to a huge range of teenage issues – sex, drugs, relationships, the lot.

Teenage Health Freak websites
www.teenagehealthfreak.org
and
www.doctorann.org
Two linked websites for young people. Catch up on the daily diary of Pete Payne, age 15 – still plagued by zits, a dodgy sex life, a pestilent sister... Jump to Doctor Ann's virtual surgery for all you want to know about fatness and farting, sex and stress, drinking and drugs, pimples and periods, hormones and headaches, and a million other things.

Other websites for teenagers

BBC kids' health
www.bbc.co.uk/health/kids

Mind Body Soul
www.mindbodysoul.gov.uk

Lifebytes
www.lifebytes.gov.uk

NSF young people's project site
www.at-ease.nsf.org.uk

Pupiline
www.pupilline.com

All these sites give lots of information about health, sex and relationships.

All your problems

ChildLine
Royal Mail Building,
Studd Street, London NW1 0QW
Freepost 1111, London N1 0BR
Tel: 020 7239 1000
Helpline: 0800 1111 (24 hours a day, every day of the year)
www.childline.org.uk
Provides a national telephone helpline for children and young people in danger or distress, who want to talk to a trained counsellor. Calls are free and confidential.

Alcohol

Drinkline

Helpline: 0800 917 8282 (9 am–11 pm,
Mon–Fri; 6 pm–11 pm, Sat–Sun)
National Alcohol Helpline – provides
telephone advice, leaflets and information
about local groups.

Bullying

Anti-Bullying Campaign

185 Tower Bridge Road, London SE1 2UF
Tel: 020 7378 1446
Gives telephone advice for young people
who are being bullied. There are also some
websites where you can get help...

Bullying Online

www.bullying.co.uk

Pupiline

www.pupilline.com

Down, depressed, anxious or suicidal

The Samaritans

Helpline: 08457 909090
www.samaritans.org.uk
Someone will always listen to you and your
problems any time of the day or night, and
it costs nothing for the call.

Drugs

National Drugs Helpline

Helpline: 0800 776600
www.ndh.org.uk
A free 24-hour, 365-day-a-year confidential
service available in English and other
languages. The helpline gives information,
advice and counselling, offering
constructive and supportive referrals and
literature to callers with concerns about
drugs and solvents.

CRIMESTOPPER SNAP – Say No And Phone CAMPAIGN

Tel: 0800 555111 (free call)
SNAP is the nationwide Crimestoppers
campaign aimed at tackling the drug
problem. You can call anonymously (you
won't be asked your name, address or phone
number) if you know anyone who regularly
supplies drugs or who commits any crime.

Release

388 Old Street, London EC1V 9LT
Advice line: 020 7729 9904
(10 am–6 pm, Mon–Fri)
24-hour emergency line: 020 7603 8654
Drugs in schools: 0345 366666
(10 am–5 pm, Mon–Fri)
www.release.org.uk
Confidential service for drug-related legal
problems. Concerned with the welfare of
users (of both illegal and prescribed drugs)
and their family and friends. Offers
emergency help in cases of arrest.

Eating disorders

Eating Disorders Association (EDA)

First Floor, Wensume House, 103 Prince of
Wales Road, Norwich NR1 1DW
Youth helpline: 01603 765050 (4–6 pm
Mon–Fri)
www.edauk.com
Youth helpline for those aged 18 years and
younger. Aims to help and support all those

affected by anorexia and bulimia, especially sufferers, the families of sufferers and other carers.

If you are ill
NHS Direct
Tel: 0845 4647
www.nhsdirect.nhs.uk
Talk to a nurse on the phone about any health problem you are worried about.

HIV/Aids
National Aids Helpline
Tel: 0800 567123 (free and confidential; available 24 hours a day, 7 days a week)
Questions or worries about Aids can be discussed with a trained adviser.

Sex and everything attached
Brook Advisory Service
Young people's helpline: 0800 0185 023
www.brook.org.uk
User-friendly information service, offering advice on sex and contraception for all young people. Will tell you all about local clinics and send you leaflets even if you are under 16.

fpa (formerly The Family Planning Association)
2–12 Pentonville Road, London N1 9FP
Tel: 020 7837 5432
Helpline: 0845 310 1334
(9 am–7 pm, Mon–Fri)
Gives information on all aspects of contraception and sexual health. Free fun leaflets available. They also run a telephone helpline for anyone who wants information on contraception and sexual health. Phone the helpline number to find the nearest fpa clinic in your area.

BAAF (British Agencies for Adoption and Fostering)
Tel: 020 7593 2000 (9 am–5 pm, Mon–Fri)
www.baaf.org.uk
A central agency for organizations involved in adoption and fostering. Publishes useful information leaflets and books about various aspects of adoption. Offers advice on tracing.

Rape Crisis Helplines
Look in the telephone directory or ring Directory Enquiries on 192 for the Helpline number in your area. Provides free confidential support and advice to victims of rape.

Lesbian and Gay Switchboard
Tel: 020 7837 7324 (24 hours a day)
www.llgs.org.uk
(this is the London and national Switchboard; there are also a number of regional Switchboards).
Offers information and advice to lesbians and gay men and their families and friends.

Smoking
QUIT
Quitline: 0800 002200 (1 pm–9 pm)
www.quit.org.uk
Want to give up smoking? Phone this line for help.

Index